DATE DUE

THE World of Kew

THE World of Kew

CAROLYN FRY

BBC BOOKS

CONTENTS

INTRODUCTION

AS THE SEASONS PASS, so too do the botanical highlights of a visit to Kew Gardens. Spring crocuses and daffodils bring long-awaited carpets of colour and the certainty that summer will soon coax beds of shrubs into bloom. When the sun is at its apex, exhibitionist rhododendrens and azaleas unleash showy profusions of pink and red, while the uplifting scents of jasmine and rose linger on the air. Only the thirsty lawns eagerly await the onset of autumn. When it comes, crimson-tinted trees take centre stage and visitors celebrate the tradition of harvest at Kew's pumpkin festival. Then, as winter winds rip away the last shrivelled leaves, the cosy Palm House imbues chill city dwellers with the sultry warmth of the Tropics and the hope that spring will come round soon.

These are the obvious glories of Kew, as seen by the one million visitors who pass through its turnstiles each year. But what about the tireless work and dedication that goes on behind the scenes and makes Kew a centre of excellence for botanical science, a renowned horticultural educator and a champion of conservation around the world? The aim of this book is to bring that unseen world to the fore and to reveal many of the fascinating and important activities that Kew staff carry out in the UK and abroad. You may chuckle at the comic sixteenth-century descriptions of medicinal plant uses on a visit to the Nosegay Garden behind Kew Palace, yet Kew scientists are finding that traditional remedies often have a basis in science. Their ground-breaking work into sage, figwort and eucalyptus is helping find treatments for diseases such as Alzheimer's, AIDS and cancer. Wander through the rock garden and you may stop to admire the delicate red and yellow flower of the lady's slipper orchid. Its presence is thanks to the painstaking work of Kew's micropropagators, whose pioneering techniques rescued the species from the brink of extinction.

Kew's modern-day roles are the legacy of a 250-year heritage. The gardens were founded in 1759, when Princess Augusta decided to plant a garden that would 'contain all the plants known on Earth'. A few trees in the gardens today, such as the stately Oriental plane (*Platanus orientalis*)

to the west of the Princess of Wales Conservatory, still date from Kew's embryonic days. As influential characters such as Sir Joseph Banks and Sir William Hooker dispatched botanists to gather exotic plants from the far reaches of the planet, the gardens grew in size and stature. Soon Kew became much more than a showcase for the world's plants. During colonial times, its experts advised the government on economically valuable species and initiated transfers of seedlings between British colonies. Some of its actions were truly world changing; its transfer of rubber seeds and seedlings from Brazil to Sri Lanka and Singapore helped launch the global rubber market that still keeps us in car tyres and condoms today.

Today, Kew is motivated by the need to conserve the world's botanic resources. It increasingly works with organisations and governments around the world to monitor and protect threatened plants. Kew scientists working in Cameroon recently discovered an area of highland forest containing more species than any part of mainland tropical Africa so far documented. They

ABOVE: Kew botanists conducting a vegetation survey on Mount Cameroon.

are now helping the government develop legislation for conserving the region. When repeated volcanic eruptions on the Caribbean island of Montserrat destroyed its botanic garden and killed swathes of tropical rainforest, Kew stepped in to assist local rangers map the remaining flora and establish a new national garden in a safer location. In all projects, the emphasis is on sharing expertise to preserve vulnerable plants and ecosystems. Seeds are constantly gathered and stored in the Millennium Seed Bank at Wakehurst Place to act as an insurance policy against changes that may affect the world's botanic resources in the future.

Closer to home, Kew uses the Natural Areas part of the botanic gardens and the Loder Valley Nature Reserve at Wakehurst Place to showcase ways of encouraging indigenous species. By reviving traditional methods of

woodland management, such as coppicing and charcoal burning, it is demonstrating that it is possible to improve biodiversity on a local scale. Rare species such as dormice are now thriving at Wakehurst and endangered stag beetles are regularly spotted around the specially created loggery at Kew. In recognition of its efforts to nurture the environment, the gardens recently became the first world heritage site to gain the ISO14001 award for sustainability. The hope is that by setting an example through its day-to-day operations Kew will also promote the need for conservation to its visitors. At a time when scientists are suggesting climate change may endanger as much as a quarter of the world's flora, Kew's scientific findings are proof that plants are not only objects of beauty to be admired as the seasons change, but are vital to the health of the planet and the future of the human race.

BELOW: Horticulturalists work from a platform to keep Kew's glasshouse displays healthy and trim.

CHAPTER 1
CREATING KEW

PREVIOUS PAGE:
What started as
a small royal
garden is today
a botanical centre
of excellence.

BELOW: A painting
showing the Nash
Conservatory
and Kew Palace
in 1898.

Cِ ENTURIES OF HISTORY lie ingrained in the weathered trees, trim lawns, blooming shrubs and exotic architecture that make up the Royal Botanic Gardens at Kew. As far back as the early seventeenth century, Henry Capel's garden at Kew Farm was said to have the 'choicest fruit of any plantation in England'. When green-fingered royals moved into the area they made gardening fashionable by decorating their estates with unusual trees and follies. In the early eighteenth century the area we know as Kew Gardens today was occupied by the two rectangular, neighbouring estates of Richmond and Kew. The former lay beside the Thames and was acquired by George, Prince of Wales, in 1718. He lived in Richmond Lodge with his wife, Caroline. The Kew estate lay to the northeast, separated from Richmond by a walled track called Foot Lane or Love Lane. It was inhabited by George's son Frederick, Prince of Wales, from 1731. Frederick lived in Capel's Farm, but renamed it the White House after extending it and facing it with white stucco.

From this period both royal households invested greatly in tree planting and landscaping, as increasing exploration of the planet wrought a fascination with exotics, and promoted the exchange of gardening ideas among Europe's aristocracy. After George ascended the throne in 1727, Queen Caroline redesigned the Richmond estate with the aid of landscape gardener Charles Bridgeman and architect William Kent. Meanwhile, Frederick and his wife, Princess Augusta, fashioned a great lawn, kitchen garden, lake and melon ground at Kew with the assistance of their friend Lord Bute, an aristocrat skilled in gardening. When Frederick died unexpectedly in 1751, Augusta continued to develop the 40 hectares (100 acres) she had inherited, and in 1759 set about creating a physic garden that would 'contain all the plants known on Earth'. In doing so, she planted the seeds for today's Royal Botanic Gardens at Kew.

ABOVE: Princess Augusta, Kew's founder, aimed to create a garden to 'contain all the plants known on Earth'.

William Aiton, a well-respected plantsman who had demonstrated his botanical prowess at Chelsea Physic Garden, came to manage the garden. Around 1.6 hectares (4 acres) in size, it displayed some 2700 species of herbaceous plants arranged in rows according to the system of classification developed by the Swedish naturalist Carolus Linnaeus. This taxonomic method for naming, ranking and classifying organisms is still in wide use today. Each genus was identified by a name tag, and every species by a number that correlated to a written record of all the herbaceous plants. The garden subsequently expanded, thanks largely to donations from amateur naturalist John Ellis.

Bute continued to be influential at Kew, advising Augusta on the garden and acting as 'finishing tutor' to her son, the future George III of England. In 1761 the plantsman Peter Collinson acknowledged Bute's input to the garden, saying: 'I shall with pleasure see your wonderful operations & the improvements those gardens have receiv'd from your great skill in every branch of science.' He also recommended him to Linnaeus, saying: 'You desire to know our botanical people: the first in rank is the Right Honourable the Earl of Bute.' Renowned gardener Thomas Knowlton declared the garden as having 'one of the best collections in the kingdom, if not the world', confirming Kew's increasing reputation as a centre of excellence for collecting, classifying and displaying plants.

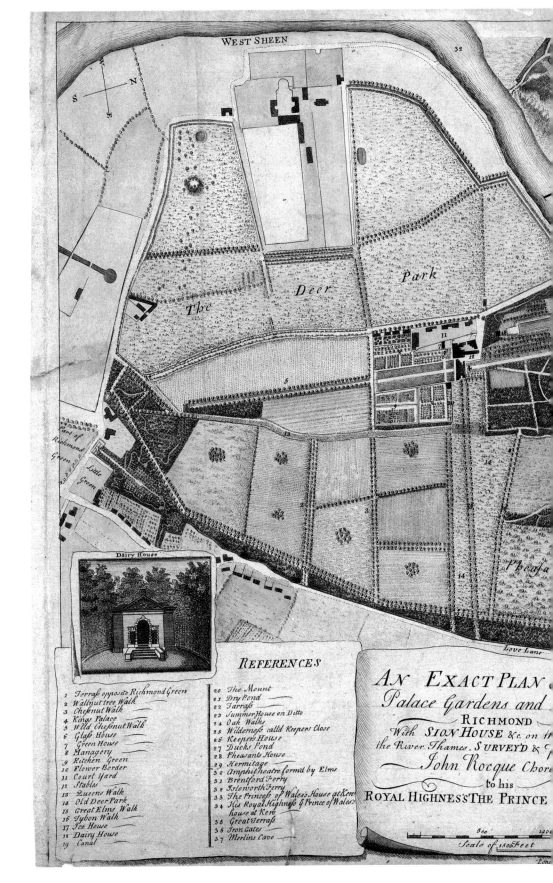

WEST SHEEN

32

Deer Park

The

Part of Richmonds Green

Little Green

Dairy House

Love Lane

Pheasa

REFERENCES

1 Terrass opposite Richmond Green
2 Wallnut tree Walk
3 Chesnut Walk
4 Kings Palace
5 Wild Chesnut Walk
6 Glass House
7 Green House
8 Managery
9 Kitchen Green
10 Flower Border
11 Court Yard
12 Stables
13 Queens Walk
14 Old Deer Park
15 Great Elms Walk
16 Sybon Walk
17 Ice House
18 Dairy House
19 Canal

20 The Mount
21 Dry Pond
22 Terrass
23 Summer House on Ditto
24 Oak Walks
25 Wilderness calld Keepers Close
26 Keepers House
27 Ducks Pond
28 Pheasants House
29 Hermitage
30 Amphitheatre formd by Elms
31 Brentford Ferry
32 Isleworth Ferry
33 The Princess of Wales's House at Kew
34 His Royal Highness the Prince of Wales's
    house at Kew
35 Great Terrass
36 Iron Gates
37 Merlins Cave

AN EXACT PLAN
Palace Gardens and
RICHMOND
With SION HOUSE &c. on tr
the River Thames. SURVEY'D &
John, Rocque Chore
to his
ROYAL HIGHNESS'S THE PRINCE

500
Scale of 150 Feet

14

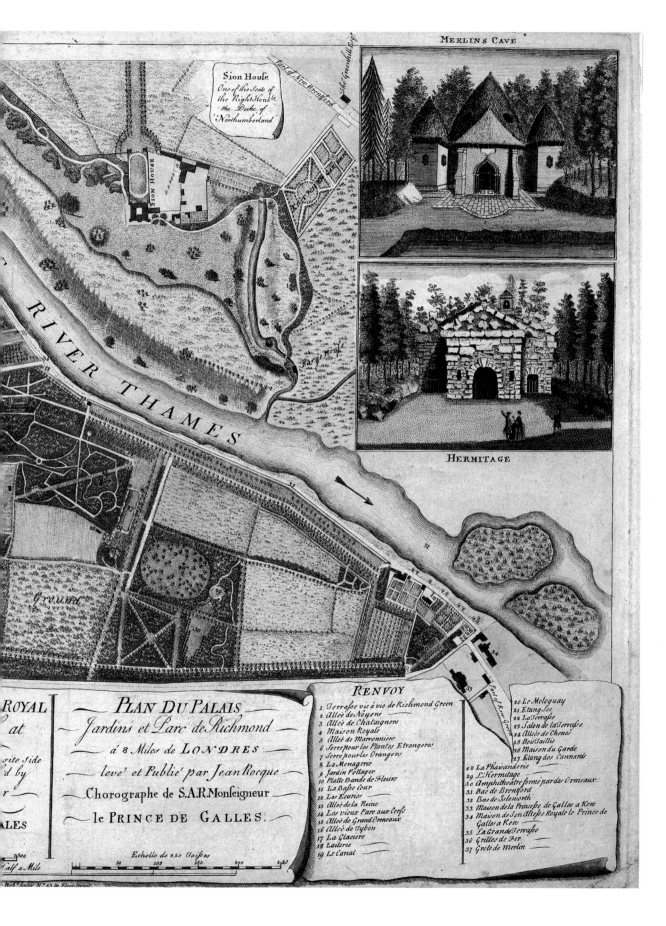

MERLINS CAVE

HERMITAGE

Sion House
One of the Seats of
the Right Honble
the Duke of
Northumberland

RIVER THAMES

PLAN DU PALAIS
Jardins et Parc de Richmond
à 8 Miles de LONDRES
levé et Publié par Jean Rocque
Chorographe de S.A.R. Monseigneur
le PRINCE DE GALLES.

Echelle de 250 Toises

RENVOY
1 Terrasse vis à vis de Richmond Green
2 Allée de Noyers
3 Allée de Chataigners
4 Maison Royale
5 Allée de Marronniers
6 Serre pour les Plantes Etrangeres
7 Serre pour les Orangers
8 La Menagerie
9 Jardin Potager
10 Platte Bande de Fleurs
11 La Basse Cour
12 Les Ecuries
13 Allée de la Reine
14 Les vieux Parc aux Cerfs
15 Allée de Grand Ormeaux
16 Allée de Tybon
17 La Glaciere
18 Laiterie
19 Le Canal
20 Le Moloquay
21 Etang See
22 La Terrasse
23 Salon de la Terrasse
24 Allée de Chenes
25 Bois Taillis
26 Maison du Garde
27 Etang des Cannards
28 La Phaisanderie
29 L'Hermitage
30 Amphitheatre formé par des Ormeaux
31 Bac de Brenford
32 Bac de Iselworth
33 Maison de la Princesse de Galles a Kew
34 Maison de Son Altesse Royale le Prince de Galles a Kew
35 La Grande Terrasse
36 Grilles de Fer
37 Grote de Merlin

Important buildings

The growing interest in far-flung destinations prompted a fashion for garden buildings with foreign architectural styles, while the desire to grow plants from warmer latitudes generated a need for hothouses in which tropical and subtropical conditions could be artificially created. From 1757 Bute had employed the young architect William Chambers at Kew to fulfil this need. The first structure Chambers worked on was the Orangery, a classical-style plant house built from brick and faced with stucco. It stood just outside Augusta's physic garden and had underfloor heating pipes fed by two furnaces in a shed behind the building. Despite politician Sir John Parnell's comments in 1769 that it was 'filled completely, chiefly with oranges which bear extremely well and large', its tiled roof, inadequate light and insufficient heat made it unsuitable for cultivating citrus fruit.

More successful was Chambers' Great Stove (actually a heated glasshouse) built in 1761, which stood within the garden. One of the largest hothouses in the country, it contained a bark stove 18 metres (60 feet) long, with a 7.5-metre (25-foot) dry

BELOW: The Orangery, one of William Chambers' early designs.

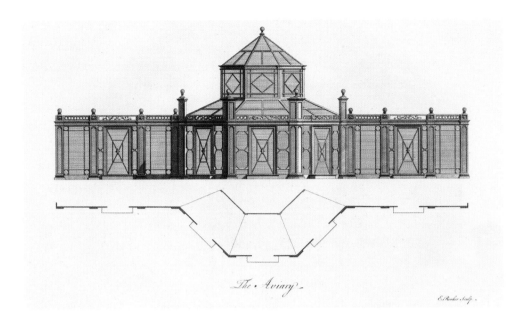

The Aviary

stove at either end. Bark stoves were a Dutch invention that came to England in the eighteenth century. Powdered oak bark mixed with elm sawdust generated enough heat to create an environment in which warmth- and moisture-loving plants could thrive. The dry stoves were used to nurture 'succulent plants which are impatient of moisture'. With knowledge still limited on which exotic plants liked dry conditions and which preferred moist ones, choosing species suited to the stoves was a matter of experimentation. The Great Stove stood for a century before being demolished. Its location, close to where the Orangery now serves as a restaurant, is marked by the aged wisteria that once grew over its eastern end.

Chambers continued working at Kew until Augusta's death in 1772. He designed at least 25 ornate garden buildings, their varied styles reflecting his ten years of classical studies in Italy and his interest in Turkish and Chinese architecture. His classical-styled buildings included the temples of Arethusa, Peace, Victory, Bellona, Pan, Aeolus and the Sun, the Gallery of Antiques and the Theatre of Augusta. While these were designed to be archaeologically correct copies of ancient constructions, his Gothic, Moorish and Chinese contributions were more frivolous. These included the Alhambra, a Moorish-style building; the Mosque, with two slender minarets and eight green stucco palm trees supporting the central dome; a 'ruined arch' folly that served as a bridge for sheep and cattle entering Kew's enclosed pastures; a Chinese-style aviary for Augusta's collection of native and foreign birds; an open-sided, Chinese-style pavilion or *T'ing*; and the high-rise Pagoda that still stands at Kew today. The last provoked much interest among local inhabitants during its construction in 1762. After seeing it from his home in Twickenham, the politician and writer Sir Horace Walpole complained to a friend that 'in a fortnight you will be able to see it in Yorkshire'.

Except for the Temple of Peace, which was never finished, all Chambers' buildings were in place by 1763. In six years he, Bute and Kew's gardeners had created a garden that was undoubtedly fit for the princess. Visitors were encouraged to take a set route around the buildings. From the White House, they passed the Orangery, then strolled into the Open Grove. At the heart of this area was the Temple of the Sun, styled on Lebanon's grand Roman remains at Baalbec. Next they encountered an enclosure divided into the Physic Garden, the Great Stove and the formal Flower Garden, complete with Augusta's aviary. A winding walk led to a menagerie, beyond which the visitors could cross a bridge to an island on a lake and shelter beneath the Chinese Pavilion. The path from the Flower Garden offered glimpses in turn of the temples of Bellona, Pan and Aeolus. From there, the House of Confucius marked the beginning of the Eastern Temple Walk, which led past a grove concealing the Theatre of Augusta and onwards to the Temple of Victory, commemorating the 1759 Battle of Minden. Its open rotunda provided a handy viewing platform for the eastern architectural delights of the Pagoda, Alhambra and Mosque, which lay towards Kew's southern boundary. Having outlived both its flanking attractions, the Pagoda reopened to the public as part of Kew's 2006 Heritage Year.

Chambers was one of the last architects employed in botanical design before professional garden designers, such as Lancelot 'Capability' Brown, came on the scene. The change led inevitably to animosity between new-school and old-school thinkers. Thomas Hardwick, an architectural student under Chambers who wrote a biography of his tutor's life, said Chambers considered 'Brown an intruder on an art in which neither his talents nor his education could entitle him to any respect'. The Kew architect certainly made no secret of the fact that he disapproved of Brown's relandscaping of the neighbouring Richmond estate in 1764, when Brown had eradicated earlier features designed by William Kent and Charles Bridgeman for Queen Caroline. It is probably fortunate that Chambers died in 1796, shortly before the Kew and Richmond estates were united. George III had sought to join the two after ascending to the throne in

The Great Pagoda.

1760 and inheriting Kew from his mother in 1772. The process took some time because an Act of Parliament and the consent of local parishes were needed before the dividing Love Lane, corresponding roughly to the Holly Walk in today's gardens, could be closed. Eventually, however, the powers that be agreed to the closure, and the boundary walls were finally demolished. In 1802 the estates of Kew and Richmond became one.

New blood

Although Lord Bute had been influential in the young George's life, he had fallen from favour by the time Augusta died, and therefore lost his consultancy role. With Kew already one of the best-stocked gardens in the country, a leader with vision was required to safeguard its reputation and shape its future. But who would be suitable? In 1768 the enthusiastic young scientist Joseph Banks had joined Captain James Cook on board HMS *Endeavour* to explore the unknown South Pacific. When the ship returned three years later, Banks brought back the first plants and artefacts from the region. His dried herbarium specimens alone yielded 1300 new species and 110 new genera. As a result, he became something of a celebrity botanist and was invited to meet George III at Richmond. Their meeting marked the start of a long friendship and Banks's involvement with Kew. Although Banks was never officially made director, William Townsend Aiton, who succeeded his father at Kew in 1793, acknowledged Banks's status when he told a reporter shortly before the two estates merged: 'This establishment is placed under the direction of Sir Joseph Banks.'

The friendship between Banks and the king grew, partly through their mutual appreciation of rural affairs. When the king learnt that he might improve the quality of wool from his British flock by cross-breeding with Spanish merinos, Banks agreed to acquire some sheep from Spain through his network of contacts, and approached a trader called Thomas March. Secrecy was important to prevent the Spanish from thinking Britain might wish to compete with them in the wool trade. In 1788 Banks hinted at the covert nature of the operation in a letter he sent March:

> In answer to your very Obliging & Friendly Letter of Augst. 18, I can only say that I most fully approve of your Plan of Obtaining Sheep, & most heartily thank you for your very Obliging and friendly assistance in a matter which occupies my

mind most fully … To depend upon a Country naturally unkindly to you for the Raw material of the finest branch [of] your Principle manufacture, & to be in hourly danger of the privilege of Obtaining it being resumd, is a humiliating Consideration to a great nation. To put her in possession of that Raw material, then, is an act deserving the best Kind of Gratitude.

ABOVE: Portraits of Sir Joseph Banks, *left*, and Captain James Cook.

March was easily able to smuggle several of the animals from Spain into Portugal and then on to Kew, where they grazed around the Pagoda. Once the flock had multiplied, some of the sheep were auctioned and ended up making the long sea voyage to New South Wales, where they helped launch Australia's merino wool industry.

Banks realized that if Kew were to compete with up-and-coming rival gardens in Paris and Vienna, he would need to rethink the way in which its plants were gathered. Until this time, the process had been largely indiscriminate, but now he sought to send collectors to specific parts of the world with strict guidelines on what to bring back. His plan was that Kew would cultivate and exchange seedlings among countries across the expanding British Empire. With lucrative commodities such as spices, tea, coffee, tobacco and sugar derived from plants, Banks realized the gardens could play a useful economic role at the same time as boosting scientific understanding of the plant kingdom. Under his direction, many botanists were sent to the outer reaches of the empire to collect plants and set up botanical gardens that would act as local offshoots of Kew. The first official collector, Francis Masson, hitched a ride with Captain Cook on HMS *Resolution* to the Cape of Good Hope in South Africa, where he sourced new species of ericas, pelargoniums, stapelas and more. Meanwhile, William Kerr gathered tiger lilies and the double yellow Banksian rose from China, before heading up a new botanical garden in Ceylon (now Sri Lanka); and Allan Cunningham and James Bowie spent time plant hunting in Brazil, before setting sail respectively for Botany Bay and the Cape of Good Hope.

Banks issued strict instructions to his roving botanists to give the plants they gathered the greatest care on their long journeys to Kew. As well as recording all plant species encountered, supplying both their Latin and local names, they were to collect and dry specimens of anything they felt worthy of bringing home, and gather ripe seeds, noting the environmental conditions in which they were found. Any valuable or unusual specimens deemed unlikely to be grown from seed at Kew were to be sent live to the gardens. Banks underlined the importance of selecting plants that had a high chance of survival, as illustrated in a communication to Cunningham and Bowie:

> We must however continually recollect that one Plant from the Cape of Good Hope or from N S Wales that will live in the dry Stove or perhaps in the Green House is worth in Kew Gardens a score of tender Plants that require the Hot house or Roaster. I trust however that some Plants may and will be found capable of Greenhouse cultivation. In all cases where you suspect a plant to be hardy you will not[e] it especially in your Journal which will be a useful memorandum for us here.

The pair clearly took their instructions to heart. Their journal entry dated 1 February 1815 reads as follows:

Wednesday. At home sorting specimens and seeds, collected yesterday, very warm and close, till about 11 o'clock A.M. when the sea breeze sprang up. In the afternoon went in search of some Seeds we expected were ripe, but these had been destroyed by cattle, got two specimens of sp. of Polygala, Cynanchum grandiflorum (Persoon), Cardiospermum sp., Bignonia sp. allied to B. fluviatilis, we had specimens of it before but being very difficult in drying, they lost all their leaves and flowers. This would be a most desirable plant in the stoves in the Royal Gardens, flowering very freely, when only $2\frac{1}{2}$ or 3 feet high.

This being the early nineteenth century, the care taken by collectors prior to dispatching plants was no guarantee of their safe arrival. Ocean journeys could take as long as six months, and the inevitable storms, salt-laden spray and insufficient watering claimed many casualties. Banks was adamant that his plants should take priority, requesting one captain to ensure that 'if any other plants except those intended for the King be taken on board, no water shall be issued to them until the King's plants shall have had their full allowance'. Young gardeners were warned to 'beware of liquor, as one drunken bout may render the whole of your care during the voyage useless, and put your character in a very questionable situation'. Such was the sickly state of some leafy newcomers to Kew that Banks set up a plant infirmary to provide intensive care for the weakest specimens. Many clearly survived, as William Aiton's three-volume *Hortus Kewensis* (*Kew Gardens*), published in 1789, listed about 5600 species. Just over 2000 were British and 1400 were European, while both North America and South Africa contributed 700. The total figure rose to 11,000 in the second edition, published between 1810 and 1813.

One successful plant-gathering mission was that undertaken by Captain William Bligh on HMS *Providence*, which carried breadfruit from the Pacific to the West Indies as food for slaves employed on the sugar plantations. On the return journey to England the empty ship was used to bring back healthy plants for Kew from Timor, Tasmania, New Guinea, Tahiti, St Vincent and Jamaica. This was a welcome result, given that the first attempt at transporting breadfruit had ended with mutiny on board Bligh's *Bounty* (see page 25). After the mutiny, Kew gardener David Nelson was cast away with Bligh and survived in a longboat before arriving safely on the island of Timor. However, he died shortly after from an inflammatory disease, believed to be the result of eating poisonous berries that he could not identify. When Bligh sailed to Tasmania in 1792 he named Nelson's Hill (called Mount Nelson today) out of respect for the gardener. Botanist Robert Brown later dedicated the genus *Nelsonia* of Acanthaceae to Nelson's memory.

Life for the Kew plant collectors was often arduous. Their long ocean journeys were uncomfortable and treacherous, many became ill with malaria or syphilis, and the indigenous peoples of the uncharted destinations at which they arrived could be hostile. While Francis Masson was on a plant-gathering mission to the Caribbean in 1779, he was caught up in an invasion of Grenada. Forcibly conscripted into the local militia, he had to swap plant collecting for defending the main town and harbour, and was captured by the French for his efforts. He lost his plant collection and was released only when Banks flexed his political muscle. When Masson moved on to St Lucia the next year, a hurricane devastated much of the island and he lost his new plant collection, equipment

BELOW: The mutiny aboard the *Bounty* by Robert Dodd. Banks's precious breadfruit trees are visible on deck.

MUTINY ON THE *BOUNTY*

During Joseph Banks's adventure with Captain James Cook on board HMS *Endeavour* between 1768 and 1771, he had encountered the breadfruit tree (*Artocarpus altilis*) in Tahiti. On his return, he praised the fruit's nutritional value and the ease with which the plant could be cultivated. Soon after, Banks's friend Valentine Morris, who owned property and slaves on St Vincent in the West Indies, wrote to him asking 'whether there was no possibility of procuring the bread tree either in seed or plant so as to introduce that most valuable tree into our American Islands'. Although various incentives were offered, no one took up the challenge.

Eventually a plea from Hinton East, receiver-general and accomplished botanist of Jamaica, prompted the government to approve a breadfruit-gathering mission. In May 1787 Banks sourced the 215-tonne *Bethia* and appointed David Nelson as the responsible gardener for the voyage with William Brown as his assistant. They had strict instructions that the plants should take precedence over everyone else: 'the Master & Crew of her must not think it a grievance to give up the best part of her accommodation for that purpose.'

Renamed HMS *Bounty* and captained by William Bligh, the ship set sail on 23 December. At first Bligh kept Banks abreast of his progress in letters written from various ports of call, but then there was a long silence for a year and a half. Eventually, a letter arrived for Banks in early 1790. In it Bligh explained that everything had been going well and the gathered plants had been flourishing until 28 April 1789, when some of his crew had turned against him.

At Dawn of Day Fletcher Christian, Officer of the Watch, Charles Churchill, Ships Corporal, Thomas Burkitt, Seaman, and several others came into my Cabbin, and while I was asleep seized and tyed my hands behind my back with a Strong Cord, and with Cutlasses and a Bayonet fixed at my breast threatned instant death if I spoke or made the least noise.

The mutineers cast Bligh and 18 others adrift in an open boat. They travelled northwest across the Pacific for six weeks until they reached Koepang in Timor, where Kew gardener David Nelson died from a fever. William Brown was among nine of the mutinous crew who ended up sailing the *Bounty* to Pitcairn Island and setting up a community with a group of Polynesian men and women.

After two months' recuperation, Bligh returned to England, where he was court-martialled and acquitted. In the 1790s Banks made him captain of HMS *Providence*, and he set out on another attempt to take breadfruit from Tahiti to the West Indies. This time the mission was successful. By the early nineteenth century breadfruit was grown throughout the British West Indies, but never became the prominent food source Banks had imagined. Nonetheless, the experience encouraged more transplants of fruit to the region. A record for 12 November 1793 notes that Kew sent several types of plant to the West Indies, including peaches, nectarines, white raspberries, morello cherries, gooseberries and greengages.

and journal. Luckily, the experience did not deter him from collecting plants, and he went on to gather new species from Portugal, Algeria, South Africa, North America and Canada. We have him to thank for introducing the bird-of-paradise flower (*Strelitzia reginae*) to the UK, which he named after George III's wife, Queen Charlotte, previously Princess of Mecklenburg-Strelitz. It was probably Masson too who collected what is today one of the world's oldest pot plants – the 231-year-old specimen of *Encephalartos altensteinii* that resides in Kew's Palm House. It has produced a cone only once at Kew, in 1819, on which occasion Sir Joseph Banks reputedly made his last visit to the gardens.

OPPOSITE: The striking bird-of-paradise flower, *Strelitzia reginae*.

Decline and recovery

When both Banks and George III died in 1820, Kew lost its two driving forces. The financial and personal support that George III had contributed was not continued by his successors George IV and William IV. The average annual expenditure of £1900 dropped to £1460 between 1828 and 1831, and again to £1277 for the period 1832–6. As Kew's plant collectors were withdrawn, the rival Horticultural Society of London began sending gardeners out on plant-gathering missions. Rumours circulated about Kew's demise. George Glenny of *Gardeners' Gazette* wrote: 'The state of the place is slovenly and discreditable, and that of the plants disgracefully dirty.' He advised Aiton, who was essentially now in charge of Kew, to 'reform – or quit'.

When William IV died and income from Hanover ceased, the Treasury reviewed the finances of the Royal Household. The royal gardens at Windsor, Hampton Court, Buckingham Palace, Kensington Palace and Kew were considered ripe for making savings. A working party under the leadership of John Lindley, professor of botany at University College London, and assistant secretary of the Horticultural Society, was asked to report on the gardens. He and his colleagues concluded that Kew should either be abandoned or developed as a national botanic garden that could provide plants and botanical advice to the colonies. 'Medicine, commerce, agriculture, horticulture, would derive considerable advantages from the establishment of such a system,' reported Lindley.

The Treasury chose to save Kew and sanctioned its transfer (minus the Royal Kitchen Garden, Kew Palace grounds and Queen Charlotte's Cottage) from the Crown to the Woods & Forests Department. In 1841 Sir William Jackson Hooker took over as director of the botanic garden, inheriting 4.4 hectares (11 acres). Incorporating a small arboretum, these were bounded to the north by the gardens of houses on Kew Green, to the east by the wall of the Royal Kitchen Garden, to the west by the lawns of Kew Palace, and to the south by the so-called Pleasure Gardens, containing the Pagoda and other follies. The ten glasshouses were in a poor state, and Chambers' Great Stove was brimming with plants from several continents. The only building with modern heating equipment was the Nash Conservatory, one of four matching buildings originally built at Buckingham Palace (another of them now houses the royal swimming pool). There was no library, and Banks's herbarium had been moved to the British Museum when he died. Clearly relishing a challenge, Hooker set about transforming Kew using Lindley's report as his basis. His goals were to achieve adequate funding, enlarge the grounds, put in place an imaginative building programme, and instigate a flexible policy that would meet both the botanical needs of scientists and the recreational wishes of the public.

From 1844 all scientific and charitable organizations had to submit regular reports of their activities and expenditure. Hooker's first one highlighted the progress he had made so far at Kew. The run-down glasshouses had been repaired and enlarged, plant collectors were once again seeking out new material for the gardens, and visitor numbers were on the rise. Hooker had also managed to get his hands on a considerable portion of the land surrounding his initial patch. William IV had given the Pleasure Gardens and Deer Park (formerly part of the Richmond estate) to his brother, the Duke of Cumberland, in 1831, but when the Duke became king of Hanover in 1837 he slowly relinquished this land. Hooker gained the Deer Park and 18 hectares (44 acres) of the Pleasure Gardens in 1844, much of the rest in 1845, and the final 3 hectares (8 acres) in 1848. Hooker had also taken charge of about 5 hectares (12 acres) in 1846, when a kitchen garden was laid out for the royal family at Frogmore. Kew now comprised over 100 hectares (250 acres). Only the grounds of Queen Charlotte's Cottage and Kew Palace were beyond the director's control. With so much more space, Hooker set about developing a bigger arboretum, and commissioned William Andrews Nesfield to design it. It is this talented formal landscape gardener that Kew has to thank for the Pagoda and Syon vistas that still define the gardens today.

Hooker had also inaugurated a library and merged his own collection of specimens with botanist George Bentham's to create an official Herbarium. Pleased at having

turned around the gardens that only a few years before had faced closure, he announced ambitious plans for a new palm house, 'a noble structure, which if carried to complete execution will be second to none in Europe'. Decimus Burton, a classical architect in his early forties, was chosen to design the new glasshouse, and presented plans for a building not dissimilar to his Great Conservatory at Chatsworth. There were worries that the central pillars would restrict the space needed for the plants, but this potential problem was avoided when ironfounder Richard Turner suggested using a 'deck beam' of wrought iron rather than cast iron, a technique borrowed from shipbuilding. As wrought iron has greater tensile strength when curved than cast iron, Turner was able to use it to span great widths unsupported by pillars. Built entirely of metal with curved panes of glass, the Palm House was completed in 1848. It was heated by coal-fired boilers located in the basement, and had a remote chimney disguised as an Italian campanile. Although no longer used for its original purpose, this stack still stands beside the Victoria Gate visitor centre today. An underground tunnel, along which coke was brought to fuel the boilers, linked the two. Hooker was delighted with his new centrepiece: 'In the Palm stove the growth and vigour of the inmates attest the excellence of the structure for cultivation, the foliage of some of the plants already exceeding 60 feet from the ground. The palms and tree ferns are among the finest ever reared in Europe.'

Plants that helped build an empire

In 1849, as the Palm House began receiving enthusiastic Victorian visitors, Hooker converted a Georgian fruitstore to form another attraction: the Museum of Economic Botany. Housing items such as clothing and musical instruments gathered by Kew's collectors over the years, the exhibits served to demonstrate to the untravelled masses the diverse uses of plants by different cultures. The country was fast becoming the most powerful nation in the world, and Hooker, like Banks before him, believed plants could play a role in helping Britain to maintain this supremacy through trade.

The Wardian case, a glazed wooden box that protected plants from the elements, was now being used to transport seedlings from abroad, and between 1843 and 1849 Kew collectors sent 92 cases of plants to the gardens. The collectors included

OPPOSITE TOP:
A Wardian case.

OPPOSITE BELOW:
Rhododendrons
at Kew.

CREATING KEW

William's son Joseph, who introduced 28 species of rhododendrons to Britain. After a two-year journey to Sikkim in Asia his collection was so great that it took him six weeks to arrange, catalogue and pack the '80 coolie loads' of specimens that he sent back to Kew. In 1855 Joseph gave up his wanderings to work as assistant to his father. With Kew now reinstated as both a leading botanic garden and visitor attraction, the pair turned their attention to a number of economic missions. Over the years they sent tea to Jamaica, mahogany plants and cork oak to India, an improved strain of tobacco to Natal in South Africa, and Liberian coffee to the West and East Indies.

The potential of plants to boost Britain's economy is demonstrated by the transplantation of tea from China to India. Working for the East India Company in

PACKING TEA IN INDIA. (INDIAN TEA ASSOCIATION).

the late 1840s, plant collector Robert Fortune supervised the transfer of 23,892 young plants and 17,000 seedlings, plus eight Chinese tea growers and their equipment, to the foothills of the Himalayas. As a result, between 1854 and 1929 the value of tea imports to Britain rose 737 per cent – from £24,000 to £200,880.

Having seen the early success of the tea transfers, in 1858 William Hooker organized an expedition to gather species of cinchona tree from four areas of the Andes. Malaria was prevalent in many of the countries that Britain now controlled, and cinchona bark contained quinine, which had proved successful in treating the disease. By establishing plantations of cinchona in India, Britain reasoned that it would no longer have to buy supplies from the South American republics where the trees grew in the wild. Hooker directed Sir Clements Markham, a geographer who went on to become president of the Royal Geographical Society, and Richard Spruce, a plant collector who collected extensively for Kew in the Amazon and Andes, along with two Kew-trained assistants, to bring him seeds from different parts of South America. Markham went to Peru and Bolivia and secured a source of yellow cinchona (*Cinchona calisaya*), while Spruce tracked down a supply of red cinchona (*Cinchona pubescens*) in Ecuador. The yellow variety was the favoured species because it had the higher quinine content, but most of the seedlings that Markham acquired died in transit. Spruce, on the other hand, managed to supply 637 seedlings and 100,000 seeds to Kew. The seedlings and seeds were nurtured at Kew in a specially prepared forcing house, then sent as seedlings in Wardian cases to the Indian Nilgiri Hills. They were cared for by William McIvor, superintendent of the Government Garden in Ootacamund, who planted them up in plantations in areas he deemed the most suitable. By 1867 these had generated 480 hectares (1200 acres) of cinchona trees in India, and further plantations in Ceylon and British Sikkim. Unfortunately for the British, the Dutch had even greater success with a species called *Cinchona ledgeriana* and a hybrid called 'crown barks', which they grew on plantations in Java. As a result, the Dutch supplied 97 per cent of the international market until World War II.

One plant transfer that proved a much greater economic success for Britain was that of rubber. Early in the nineteenth century rubber was used to waterproof cloth, make elastic bands and provide durable boots. However, the material had its flaws: it became rigid when cold, pliable when warm, and also tended to deteriorate, particularly when exposed to the sun. Then the American Charles Goodyear discovered that rubber could be stabilized by mixing it with sulphur while heated, and its range of possible uses multiplied overnight. Whereas Britain had imported just 211 kilograms (464 pounds) of crude rubber in 1830, by 1857 that figure stood at 10,000 kilograms (98 tonnes), and 1874 levels were just under six times as much again. This would have been good news for Brazil, where rubber was harvested from wild trees, had Britain not sought to establish its own plantations. After investigating which varieties were likely to produce the highest yield, in 1873 the India Office posted a request to the consul in Belém, then capital of Brazil's eastern province of Pará, for seeds of *Hevea brasiliensis*. Joseph Hooker, who had now taken over the directorship of Kew from his father, was notified of the request and gave word that he was prepared for their arrival and distribution. Some three years passed before a successful transfer was made by Henry Alexander Wickham, who gathered seeds from Seringal on the Tapajós River and sent them by boat to Kew.

A series of letters, retained in the archives at Kew, records the path of the seeds from Brazil to Ceylon. One, dated 29 January 1876, from Wickham to Hooker, reads: 'I am just about to start for the Curinga districts in order to get you as large a supply of the fresh Indian rubber seeds as possible.' The next, a note written at Kew on 7 July of the same year, confirms:

BELOW: Gathering tea leaves in China.

70,000 seeds of Hevea brasiliensis were received from Mr H.A. Wickham on June 14th. They were all sown the following day and a few germinated on the fourth day after. Up to this date 2,700 have been potted off ... This may be considered the total number of plants to be obtained, as very few will germinate after this date. Many are now 15 inches high and all are in rigorous health.

BELOW: Rubber is tapped from trees by slicing the bark diagonally to let the latex drain out.

Next up comes an estimate of the cost of sending 2000 plants of *Hevea* from Kew to Ceylon. It quotes '40 Wardian cases @ £3.00: £120.00; Man to Colombo and back: £63.00; Carrier to London: £7.00; contingencies: £10.00.' The final part of the story is a letter dated 16 September 1876, from the Royal Botanic Garden Peradeniya, Ceylon: 'My dear Hooker, You will be rejoiced to hear that the Heavea [sic] and castilloa plants have arrived in very fair order indeed. 90 per cent will then little doubt be saved of the Heavea [sic] collection and we have 28 out of the 31 castilloas looking green and promising ... '

Although the introduction of rubber to Ceylon was a success and the trees bore seeds, there was not much demand for them initially. No one was yet sure what conditions best suited the plants, and as they took five years to become established plantation managers felt it was too risky to switch from growing coffee to rubber without further investigation. In 1877, however, some 22 plants were shipped from Ceylon to Singapore and were soon thriving. When a new superintendent, Henry W. Ridley, arrived to take over the garden in Singapore he made it his business to conduct large-scale scientific experiments into rubber. Ridley had been trained at Kew under Sir Joseph Hooker, and wasted no time in raising 8000 new plants. He then carried out tests to discover what tapping methods were the most effective, how seeds could best be stored during transport, and whether disease might affect plants sliced open by tapping. He discovered that frequent tapping carried out in the morning produced the highest yields of latex, that fresh seeds packed in damp charcoal travelled well over moderate distances, and that fears about gashes encouraging disease were unfounded. His findings helped stimulate a trade in seeds on the Malay Peninsula. By 1899 over a million young plants derived from seeds grown at Kew were thriving there, and in the decade that followed 400,000 hectares (1 million acres) of land came under rubber cultivation. The majority of rubber trees grown today can be traced back to seedlings propagated by Kew.

Expanding in all directions

Leaving out the disease germs that fill the air of the East End, consider but the one item of smoke. Sir William Thistleton-Dyer, curator of Kew Gardens, has been studying smoke deposits on vegetation, and, according to his calculations, no less than six tons of solid matter, consisting of soot and tarry hydrocarbons, are deposited every week on every quarter of a square mile in and about London. This is equivalent to twenty-four tons per week to the square mile, or 1248 tons per year to the square mile.

Jack London, *The People of the Abyss* (1903)

When William Thistleton-Dyer succeeded Sir Joseph Hooker in 1885, he emphasized Kew's function in boosting colonial economies. He published the results of the gardens' plant transfers in the new *Kew Bulletin*, making Kew a centre for economic intelligence. As Britain gained control of new lands in Africa, Kew set up new botanic gardens to experiment with agricultural crops and other plant-based economic resources. Seed sent from the West Indies initiated the cocoa industry in the Gold Coast (now Ghana), rubber grown in Zanzibar yielded rubber sales of £200,000 in 1891, and Gambia thrived on its groundnut exports.

By the early twentieth century, some 160 Kew-trained botanists were working in senior posts across Asia, Africa, Australia and the USA, along with others recommended by Kew's director. Whenever the India, Colonial or Foreign Office had a botanical query, they relied on Kew's help. Joseph Chamberlain, in his role as colonial secretary, acknowledged this formally in the House of Commons, saying:

> I do not think it is too much to say that at the present time there are several of our important Colonies which owe whatever prosperity they possess to the knowledge and experience of, and the assistance given by, the authorities at Kew Gardens. Thousands of letters pass every year between the authorities at Kew and the Colonies, and they are able to place at the service of these colonies not only the best advice and experience, but seeds and samples of economic plants capable of cultivation in the colonies.

BELOW: Decimus Burton's Museum No. 1 now houses the Plants + People exhibition.

The widening of Britain's interests abroad had a direct influence on the number of specimens and artefacts being sent back to the gardens. Only a few years after the Museum of Economic Botany had opened in the building that now houses Kew's School of Horticulture, its ten rooms, passages and corners were overflowing with

items. As a result, a second museum opened in 1857 in a dedicated building facing the pond and Palm House. Confusingly, this became known as Museum No. 1, while the original one was called Museum No. 2. Two other museums were established in the following years, both devoted to timber. Museum No. 3 was located in Cambridge Cottage, a building at the northeast end of the gardens. It originally displayed exhibits devoted to British forestry, but is now used as an art gallery. Museum No. 4 was located in the Orangery and housed timber artefacts. Major donations swelled Kew's collections over the years. These included specimens from the Great Exhibition in the Crystal Palace at Hyde Park in 1851, and 4000 specimens from the India Museum in South Kensington.

Dried plant specimens also came to Kew from across the empire. In 1899, in a note to the Office of Works, the department that had assumed responsibility for the gardens, Thistleton-Dyer wrote: 'I cannot control the expansion of Kew Herbarium because I cannot control the expansion of the Empire. The scientific investigation of new territories follows their accretion.' In 1902 a new wing was built to reduce the crowding; this enabled the original wing to be gutted and fireproofed the following year.

ABOVE: The Palm House was popular with Victorian visitors.

IN KEW'S ARCHIVES: **Deadly musical instrument**

One of Kew's most prolific plant collectors was Richard Spruce. During the latter half of the nineteenth century he spent 15 years in the Amazon and Andes of South America gathering thousands of specimens of flowering plants, ferns, mosses, liverworts and lichens. He was also a prolific writer, and made copious notes about the terrain he passed through, the people he met and the plants he discovered. His friend Matthew Slater observed: 'Whether in a native hut on the Rio Negro or in his little cottage in Yorkshire, his writing-material, his books, his microscope, his dried plants, his stores of food and clothing – all had their proper place where his hand could be laid upon them in a moment. It was this habit of order, together with his passion for thoroughness in all he undertook, that made him so admirable a collector.'

As well as plant specimens, Spruce collected more than 250 items fashioned from plants, which are now held in Kew's Economic Botany Archive. These include ceremonial clothing from the Cubeú Indians, musical instruments from Rio Uaupés, weapons such as poisoned arrows and medicines used by the Manhe Indians. A project carried out between 2002 and 2005 by Kew, the Natural History Museum in London and the University of San Marcos in Lima, Peru, located artefacts held in their collections, linked these to his notes and diary entries, and made the descriptions and images available online as a resource for historians, botanists and other specialists.

One of the most unusual items collected by Spruce was a *jurupari* or devil sacred musical instrument (see below). This comprises a tube made of paxiuba (*Socratea exorrhiza*) wrapped in a long strip of bark from the walaba tree to form a type of trumpet. Spruce noted that the *jurupari*, used at ceremonial feasts, was greatly respected among its tribal users, and that no woman was ever permitted to see one; those who did – even accidentally – would be killed by poison. Youths could not touch the instrument before they had reached puberty and undergone a series of fastings. In Spruce's diaries he explains: 'The Juruparis are kept hidden in the bed of some stream deep in the forest, in which no one dares to drink or bathe; and they are brought out only at night and blown outside the house where the feast is held, in order that no women may obtain a sight of them.'

Thistleton-Dyer also made other improvements to Kew. He removed the fence that had until then separated the true Physic or Botanic Garden from the Pleasure Gardens, restructured the Arboretum and created a bamboo garden and a sunken rose garden from reclaimed gravel pits. During his time as Joseph Hooker's assistant, he had designed a rock garden to display 3000 donated alpine plants; now, as director, he commissioned a dedicated Alpine House, which opened in 1887. He also founded the Jodrell Laboratory, recognizing Kew's importance in scientific plant research. To please the public, Kew opened its first refreshment pavilion and, after a debate in the House of Commons and a prolonged campaign in the press that began in Hooker's day, agreed to allow visitors in from 10 a.m. rather than midday during the summer.

Twentieth-century changes

The first three women gardeners arrived at Kew from the Horticultural College for Women at Swanley, Kent, in 1896. A stickler for uniforms, Thistleton-Dyer insisted they wear clothing unlikely to distract their male colleagues. As a result, they undertook their digging, weeding and watering in brown bloomers, woollen stockings, waistcoat, jacket and peaked cap. In 1913 women again became the centre of attention at Kew when suffragettes attacked three orchid houses, then later burnt down the refreshment pavilion. The *Gardener's Magazine* had little sympathy for the women's desire to vote, saying: 'An attack on plants is as cowardly and cruel as one upon domestic animals or those in captivity.' During both world wars, male domination at Kew was reversed as women took the place of men called up to fight. To see women working in this way was such an anomaly that they were featured in an article in May 1942 in the *The Illustrated London News* (the article was entitled 'Girls take over at Kew') and given the nickname 'Kewties'.

With commodities sourced from Europe no longer obtainable, Kew took on a new role during the conflicts. The government called on the gardens' scientists to advise it on alternative sources of food, intensive farming methods and medicinal plants. In particular, Kew experimented with several varieties of rose hip, a rich source of vitamin C. Between 1941 and 1945, on the advice of Kew's medicinal plant expert, Dr Ronald Melville, volunteers harvested nearly 2000 tonnes of hips, producing

CREATING KEW

10 million bottles of rose-hip syrup. Kew also agreed to cultivate those pharmaceutical plants that were unprofitable for commercial growers. In 1941 it harvested a tonne of shoots of deadly nightshade (*Atropa belladonna*) for potential use as an antidote to the nerve gas produced by the Germans.

The role of rebuilding Kew after World War II fell initially to Edward Salisbury, who became director in 1943. Some 30 high explosives had fallen in the gardens, breaking glass and damaging plants. The Palm House was deemed unsafe for the public, and serious thought was given to replacing it with a design incorporating the arches that had spanned the Mall during the Queen's coronation. Fortunately, the Ministry of Works, originally the Office of Works, opted instead to repair it.

The gardens gained a new building when the Australian government commemorated the director's visit to the Antipodes in 1949 with the gift of a large glasshouse. Its steeply pitched roof was designed to allow in the maximum amount of light, and it was dedicated to displaying Australian flora. Now named the Evolution House, it houses a permanent exhibition tracing 3500 million years of plant development.

Although the British Empire was unravelling during the post-war years, Kew was still transferring plants, such as food crops, from Peru and Bolivia to East Africa. In 1951 Salisbury commissioned a dedicated Quarantine House in which to hold plants awaiting transfer abroad. Plants of proven economic use, such as bananas, rubber and cocoa, were propagated here and sent to research institutes in the colonies.

By the 1960s Kew was running out of space in which to exhibit the full diversity of the world's flora. The new director, Sir George Taylor, was considering how he might solve this conundrum when the

OPPOSITE: Sunlight filters through the tropical foliage of the Palm House.

BELOW: During both world wars women 'Kewties' stepped in to replace male gardeners called up to fight.

opportunity came up for Kew to manage the National Trust-owned estate of Wakehurst Place in the High Weald of Sussex. Gerald Loder, who owned the property, had begun planting exotic trees and shrubs on the estate when he bought it in 1902, and his work was continued by its later owners, Sir Henry and Lady Price. When Kew leased the estate from the National Trust in 1965 it supplemented the already diverse range of plants by moving major collections of rhododendrons, maples, southern beeches and birches from west London. The more moisture-retentive and varied soil types, higher rainfall and sheltered, frost-free places meant gardeners could successfully grow plants at Wakehurst that did not thrive at Kew. It also enabled Kew to take a hands-on approach to conservation as the world began to wake up to the idea that prime habitats and potentially valuable plants were beginning to disappear. Now known as Kew's country home, the estate encompasses a mansion built in 1590 for Edward Culpeper, formal gardens, the 60-hectare (150-acre) Loder Valley Nature Reserve and the Francis Rose Reserve and Site of Special Scientific Interest.

Sir George also made improvements to the gardens, refurbishing the Palm House, commissioning a new wing for the Herbarium and building a new Jodrell Laboratory. He also created the Queen's Garden behind Kew Palace when the former royal residence was refurbished. The garden was designed in a late-seventeenth-century style, using only those plants that would have been available for cultivation before 1700. Sir George was clearly as interested in the practical side of gardening as the managerial demands of Kew. In his own garden at Rickmansworth he experimented with trying to grow rare and difficult plants, but, according to a report in the *Observer*, was equally adept at growing weeds. 'Following a farm walk, he turned out his trouser turn-ups and raised no fewer than 300 plants from the bits,' it reported. 'Among them were 20 different kinds of weeds. Now we know how weeds spread.' Sir George was also a member of the oddly named Committee for Beauty, a group formed by the government to recommend suitable routes and landscaping for new roads. 'We only plant trees that are indigenous to that particular part of the countryside where the road is built,' explained Sir George in an article in *Reader's Digest* in 1968.

Conservation and community

Worries about urbanization damage and the urge to start promoting conservation began to motivate Kew's activities in the 1970s. When Sir Ghillean Prance took the helm in 1988, he inspired Kew to focus on serving the needs of the world community by supporting research on conservation and the sustainable use of plants. He expanded the Jodrell Laboratory, established the Millennium Seed Bank at Wakehurst Place for seeds of threatened species, and acquired the International Mycological Institute's building in 1994. He also led many botanical expeditions to the forests of the Brazilian Amazon, providing a valuable insight into the need to conserve habitats. The Brazil nut (*Bertholletia excelsa*) is of major economic significance to the Amazon, but its survival depends on a delicate web of ecological interdependencies. Prance realized that female euglossine bees pollinate it, but will mate only with males who successfully gather scents from several orchid species that grow only in undisturbed forest. His work revealed the importance of biodiversity to the survival of many species.

Today conservation and education have become Kew's overriding goals. In the Micropropagation Laboratory staff are successfully propagating plants that have become so rare that only a solitary specimen remains. In the Jodrell Laboratory, work is under way to ensure medicinal ingredients are taken from sustainable sources. And at Wakehurst Place seeds are being stockpiled in preparation for future extinctions caused by human-induced changes to the planet's natural systems. Where in the past Kew translocated plants between countries for the economic gain of the empire, today it works in partnership with national organizations to help promote sustainable local economies and encourage conservation. In recognition of the importance of the gardens' contribution to botanical science and heritage since 1759, in 2003 Kew was awarded the status of a UNESCO World Heritage Site. Three years on, it dedicated 2006 as its Year of Heritage to celebrate the many people who have made the gardens what they are today. A specially commissioned mural, temporarily housed in the Princess of Wales Conservatory, immortalizes some of Kew's most influential characters. Sir William Hooker is there, depicted with the tabby cat that saved many a Herbarium specimen from mice; Sir Ghillean Prance holds a Brazil nut, the focus of his research; and William Andrews Nesfield leans on a wall surveying his formal landscapes. To the far left of the painting is Princess Augusta, who laid the foundations for the Kew Gardens we know today when she began creating a physic garden to 'contain all the plants known on Earth'.

GROWING REMEDIES

TUCKED AWAY BEHIND KEW PALACE at the back of the Nosegay Garden during 2006 was a small, square, open-sided building. Inside stood a wooden bench with cream cushions, a low table and various books on Britain's native flora. For several months the building was the focus of Kew's Remembered Remedies programme, an initiative aiming to record how British plants have been used as medicines over the centuries. The hope was that passers-by would stop for a few moments and write down remedies they had found effective, or that they recalled their mother or grandmother using. If their memories failed them, the cleansing scent of lavender wafting from bunches hung high on the walls could have helped. Treatment for memory loss is just one of the many uses that has been noted for this sweet-smelling ornamental plant down the years. One visitor from Northumberland filled in one of the blank cards on the table, recalling the use of dock leaves to treat nettle stings. 'Rub leaves on affected part, no preparation needed,' instructs the card. 'This is known by country persons, but the younger generation seems to have forgotten it.' They clearly need some lavender.

The Nosegay Garden, in which the Remembered Remedies booth stood during the Heritage Festival, is a reminder that painkilling tablets and contraceptive pills are modern luxuries. The garden is planted only with those shrubs and herbs that would have been available in the seventeenth century. At that time garden plants were grown primarily for food, for use as nosegays to disguise bad smells, or as medicines. Two pioneering botanists, John Parkinson (apothecary to James I) and John Gerard (superintendent of the gardens of William Cecil, adviser to Elizabeth I) wrote important books on medicinal plants during the sixteenth and seventeenth centuries. Quotes from these volumes are written on the name tags that accompany each plant in the garden. According to Parkinson's 1640 tome *Theatrum Botanicum*, which described over 3800 plants, the grape vine (*Vitis vinifera*) 'easeth those places that are bruised by falls or otherwise and curest the bite of scorpions'. The tag taken from the 1633 edition of Gerard's *Herball or Generall Historie of Plantes* says of the male fern (*Dryopteris filix-mas*): 'The roots being drunke in mede driveth forth long flat worms from the bellie.' In those days, finding which plants were effective was a matter of experimentation. Pity the person who yielded the information given by

Parkinson on the blue helmet flower (*Aconitum napellus*): 'The symptoms are these, their lips and toong [tongue] swell forthwith, their eies [eyes] hang out, their thighs are stiff and their wits are taken from them.'

New from old

While these plant uses may seem quaint and amusing, there is often more than a grain of truth in such folklore. The history of medicine as a science dates back to Hippocrates, who lived in Greece between 460 and 377 BC. Among his writings on remedies, he noted that the use of powder made from the bark and leaves of the willow tree helped to heal headaches, pains and fevers. More than 2000 years later, in 1828, scientists discovered salicin, the compound in willow plants that provides the pain relief. And a decade on, an Italian chemist working at the Sorbonne in Paris split salicin into a sugar and an aromatic component (salicylaldehyde) and converted the latter, by hydrolysis and oxidation, to an acid of crystallized colourless needles. It is a refined form of this salicylic acid that is the active ingredient in aspirin tablets we take to relieve pain today.

BELOW: Sage, *Salvia offinalis*, has long been used as a treatment for memory loss.

Kew is actively involved in finding new medicines by investigating compounds found in a range of plants. One that appears promising is sage, which may have the potential to alleviate symptoms of Alzheimer's disease, a type of dementia. Interestingly, as the name tag that identifies the variegated leaves of small sage (*Salvia officinalis*) in the Nosegay Garden shows, Gerard reported in 1633 that the plant was 'singular good for the head and braine; it quickneth the sences and memory'.

Kew has always been interested in the uses of plants. As well as simply procuring plants and seeds, Sir Joseph Banks's plant collectors were instructed: 'At all places where a friendly intercourse with the Natives is established, you are to make diligent inquiry into their manners, Customs, Language and Religion, & to obtain all the information in your power concerning their Manufactures, particularly the Art of dying [sic], in which the savages have frequently been found to excel … '

Research into drugs

An early plant of interest to Britain for its medicinal potential was cinchona, a source of quinine. In 1860 quinine was the only effective treatment for malaria, and Britons beset by disease and civil disorder in India wanted to secure their own supplies rather than rely on diminishing natural sources in Ecuador. The great plant collector Richard Spruce was therefore dispatched to Ecuador on behalf of the India Office and Kew, and secured 637 seedlings and 100,000 seeds of the red bark tree, *Cinchona pubescens*. These duly gave rise to plantations in India, Ceylon and British Sikkim. Cinchona bark remains a major source of quinine and its numerous alkaloids – bitter-tasting compounds containing nitrogen – to this day. Meanwhile, its use as a flavouring ingredient in tonic water (once medicinal) still accounts for nearly half the harvest. A promising new drug for the treatment of malaria is qinghaosu, isolated from wormwood (*Artemisia annua*). In China, tea made from the plant has been used for about 2000 years for treating malaria and fever.

Another plant that Kew was historically involved in researching for its medical properties was coca (*Erythroxylum coca*), which yields the now illicit drug cocaine. As far back as 1580, the Spanish physician Nicholas Monardes wrote of the native uses of the coca plant in a book now residing in Kew's library. In it he describes

ABOVE: Cinchona plants were cultivated at Kew and shipped to colonial plantations to provide supplies of the malarial treatment quinine.

ABOVE: The coca plant, *Erythroxylum Coca*, from which the drug cocaine was synthesized.

methods of using coca while travelling, one of which involved chewing little balls of the leaves mixed with lime made from shells. He noted: 'For the use of these litle Balls taketh the hunger and thirst from them: and they say that they receive substance thereby, as though they did eat meate.'

Reports by later travellers Alexander von Humboldt and Johann Jakob von Tschudi confirmed coca's restorative properties. Von Tschudi reported that it greatly assisted respiration and enabled him to climb high mountains without fatigue. The reports prompted widespread interest in the coca plant. The first accurate drawing appeared in the press in 1835 by none other than Kew's later director Sir William Hooker.

The interest sparked a race to discover coca's active ingredient, which was won in 1860 when chemistry student Albert Niemann isolated the alkaloid 'kokain'. Later, the Austrian ophthalmologist Karl Koller discovered that the compound had useful medicinal potential as an anaesthetic. Meanwhile, interest in the herbal coca-leaf mirrored that in the 'scientific' cocaine. A drink composed of coca and Bordeaux wine, called *vin Mariani*, gained popularity, as did a non-alcoholic equivalent, Coca-Cola, launched in 1886.

In 1869 Kew had begun cultivating coca plants from seeds donated by a Mr Abraham Dixon, who had obtained them from the Bishop of Huánaco. These yielded hundreds of plants. Twenty years later an article in the *Kew Bulletin* reviewed their progress. It noted that the annual report of the Botanic Gardens Ceylon for the year 1887 stated ' ... coca plants at Peradeniya and possibly all the plants now in the Colony had been derived from a Kew plant received in 1870'. Coca plants cultivated in Jamaica and St Lucia were also presumed to have come from the Kew plant.

In 1983 the Royal Pharmaceutical Society of Great Britain donated a vast collection of plant-related *materia medica* (materials used for medicines) to Kew. The hoard included 10,000 crude drug specimens representing medicines in use between 1800 and 1950, a large collection of microscope slides, the society's Herbarium of British and Medicinal Plants, and an extensive collection of cinchona (quinine) barks used in the treatment of malaria.

One of the highlights of the collection, now residing in the Economic Botany Archive in Kew's Banks Building, is a cabinet crammed with over 700 glass bottles of coloured essential oils dating back to the nineteenth century (see below). They include sandalwood (*Santalum album*) oil prepared in India in 1887; turmeric (*Curcuma longa*) oil; bergamot oil made from the green peel of the *Citrus bergamia* fruit; citron-scented gum (*Corymbia citriodora*) oil; and oil from myrrh (*Commiphora myrrha*).

Essential oils are those oils in plants that give them their characteristic scents. Found in many different parts of the plant, they are extracted by various methods, including compression, distillation with steam and maceration. The oils are then used in perfumes, skin preparations and flavourings, and to promote certain moods, such as happiness or calmness. As the oils in Kew's collection are known to be particularly pure, they are used as standards against which to authenticate essential oils on the market today.

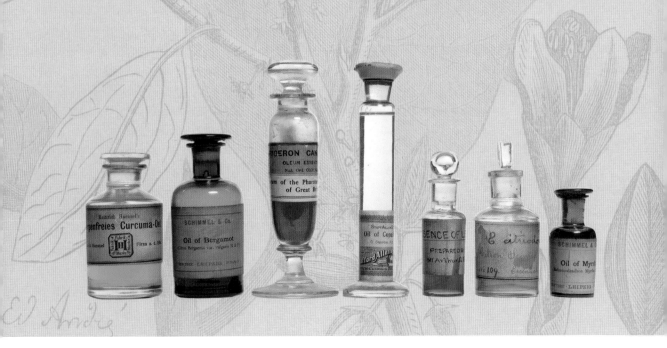

The report explored the known varieties of coca, discussed the climatic conditions best suited to the plants and noted that, unlike tea – where young leaves were harvested – mature plants produced higher yields of the alkaloids that made coca a marketable product. 'At that time coca was an acceptable drug, and cocaine was a drug of high society,' says Monique Simmonds, who works in Kew's Jodrell Laboratory. 'Coca used to be in the armed forces' chocolates until quite recently, to give them that extra buzz. And it was the hidden ingredient in Coca-Cola until early in the twentieth century. Kew has had a long history of finding out where the highest sources of an active ingredient are.'

Under the microscope

Monique coordinates the work of two groups in the Jodrell Laboratory – the Biological Interactions Section and the Centre for Economic Botany. The former group studies secondary compounds in plants. While all living organisms contain primary biochemicals that support vital life processes, certain plant groups also accumulate a range of secondary compounds that help them deter predators, attract pollinating organisms and inhibit the growth of competing plant species. Many plants containing such compounds are effective as medicines or pesticides. Today's chemists are continually searching for clues that may lead them to the medicines and crop-protection agents of the future. 'We do an awful lot of ethnobotanical type work, going out and studying what plants people are using and then, with their permission, bringing that information into the lab,' says Monique. Meanwhile, staff in the Centre for Economic Botany document the uses of plants and create databases so that the information is safely stored and made available for future research. Initially, this group was located in the Banks Building, but in 2006 a £6 million extension to the Jodrell Laboratory meant that all Monique's staff came together to work under one roof.

On a tour of the lab she explains how scientists go about looking for useful secondary compounds. One shelf holds glass columns of liquid containing broken-up plant material, such as horse chestnut flowers and grasses. This is the first stage, where leaves or flowers are broken down physically and placed in a solvent, such as water or alcohol. Traditional medicines would often be little more than an infusion of this kind to be drunk as a tincture or applied directly to the relevant part of the body. The second stage of analysis involves taking the extract and separating out different components of it using column chromatography. This is essentially a glass column with a tap at the base. Such equipment is quite old-fashioned, but can be used effectively in countries where there is no access to high-tech laboratory facilities. A solid, such as silica gel, is placed at the base of the column, then the sample is added, and a solvent introduced. As components in the sample pass through the system at different rates, they become separated, like runners at the start of a marathon. The result is that different compounds become separated into different coloured bands. 'It's just like if you drop ink on to blotting paper – you see that as it spreads out, it changes colour,' says Monique. 'In this column you can see the material has separated out into a white band, a green band and a brown band. Next we would test each layer to find out if it's the white, green or brown band that contains compounds that cause the reported medicinal activity.'

More refined testing takes place downstairs in a room full of humming, high-tech equipment. Here the various extracts are injected into a machine called a liquid chromatography mass spectrometer. This analyses the composition of material introduced to it and prints out a graph displaying peaks correlating to the percentages of the different compounds present. By noting the chemicals and where clusters of peaks are concentrated, the scientists can work out which part of their sample is of most interest. They can then run further separations to narrow down the cocktail of compounds until they isolate the one responsible for the activity in which they are interested. This might be a compound responsible for anti-inflammatory, anti-bacterial or anti-viral behaviour, for example.

Choosing plants to study

To narrow down the search for useful plants, scientists look for clues that suggest a plant might yield active compounds. Sometimes a plant will be known to be an effective remedy, and the staff will test other plants related to it to see if they may also have medicinal properties. One study is currently evaluating plants in the Myrtaceae (eucalyptus) family, for example.

In some cases a plant may be renowned for a medicinal use, but there is no known explanation for it, so staff will look for compounds that could scientifically explain that activity. In recent years Kew has discovered plant compounds that may help to combat HIV, malaria and cancer.

'We've been successful in helping to identify active plants because of our knowledge of plant chemistry and the role different plants play in their ecology,' Monique explains. 'Plants haven't evolved these compounds to provide us with medicines; they've done so to stop themselves being eaten, or to protect themselves against the sun. If we have that knowledge, we can use it to predict how a particular plant might have some medicinal use. For example, some of the compounds have potent components that repel insects. We might look at how they do that and find that they stimulate neurons in insects' taste systems. Then we'll investigate how they do that, and find that the insects have different types of receptors and that the compounds from the plant affect the creatures' potassium and calcium ion channels. Having that information would lead us to ask, "If they can do that with the ion channels in insects, have they got the potential to do it in humans?" If so, we might be able to relate the activity to different diseases where you have an ion imbalance.

'One of the leads we've been following to find medicines effective against cancer and HIV is a group of compounds that affects the utilization of sugars. Human cells have an outer layer comprised of proteins with carbohydrates (sugars) on the end. We've found that some plant compounds interact with the sugar part. With HIV or a virus, you need to have cell-to-cell recognition before a virus will be able to go from one cell to another. As these compounds affect the different sugars, they stop that cell-to-cell recognition, so the virus can't make that jump. If you then look at viral infections in plants, you find some plants are able to defend themselves, while others can't. Using that information in a lateral way, you can target discovery programmes.'

What can be learnt from British plants?

OPPOSITE: Oil from the eucalyptus tree is commonly used in decongestants, but tests at Kew may find additional medicinal uses.

Since 2000, Kew's work investigating the medicinal properties of British plants has yielded some interesting findings. The British Medicinal Plant Appeal was launched to complement the Millennium Seed Bank's aims to find and store seeds from all native British flora (it also plans to have collected 10 per cent of the world's flora by 2010). 'I did a trawl through the existing literature and found that British plants hadn't been looked at very much in recent years,' explains Monique. 'There had been

so many advances in our understanding of diseases and in molecular biology and the analytical techniques we use in the lab that I thought we should test some of those plants that people say have certain medicinal activity.'

So far the scientists have tested 100 plants and found out something new about 70 of them – either discovering a compound that was not previously known, or finding compounds in plants not thought to contain them. One plant, figwort, is proving to be particularly interesting. In his seventeenth-century book *The Complete Herbal*, Nicholas Culpeper describes the use of figwort for cleansing the system and treating 'the king's evil [tuberculosis of the lymph gland], or any other knobs, kernels, bunches

or wens growing in the flesh wheresoever; and for the haemorrhoids'. The 'king's evil' was also called scrofula, and figwort's Latin name, *Scrophularia nodosa*, reflects this. The purple-flowered inhabitant of Britain's woods and meadows was used as recently as the 1930s in rural Norfolk to treat wounds and sores. In collaboration with scientists at University College London, Kew has isolated figwort compounds called iridoids, which stimulate fibroblasts – cells in the blood associated with wound healing. The plant also contains compounds with anti-bacterial and anti-fungal properties, which increase the chances of wounds healing. 'We're hoping to do more work on these different compounds in a clinical trial setting,' says Monique.

BELOW: Three sculptures of giant seeds adorn the Millennium Seed Bank at Wakehurst Place.

The real thing?

Not all the work of the Jodrell team involves isolating unknown compounds; sometimes their knowledge is used simply to prove the presence or absence of certain plant ingredients. In the past five years they have carried out 5000 such authentications. One use of testing is in the field of traditional Chinese medicine (TCM), where similar-looking plants are sometimes substituted for the intended ingredient. Often this is because the correct plants have been overexploited and are becoming difficult or expensive to get hold of. Although a certain amount of interchange is allowed in the preparation of Chinese medicines, there have been instances where non-allowable plants have been included. For example, potato or dahlia bulbs have been used instead of tubers from orchids that have a specific medicinal function. 'Potatoes might not do you any harm, but they won't give you the medicinal properties you would expect to get,' says Monique. 'My colleague Chris Leon is writing a book that will outline the main plants, especially those encountered in the UK TCM trade, and will compare

BELOW: Plants used in Traditional Chinese Medicine are sold in markets across Asia.

substitutes that you might get. It will present morphological features that can be used to identify the main plant and also the substitutes, along with conservation assessments. Having a better idea about the conservation assessment of those particular species will give us an idea of whether we are likely to face an increase in adulterants in future.'

Authentication has also been effective in testing the provenance of essential oils, such as sandalwood, which has soothing and anti-bacterial properties on the skin. There are 104 names that can legitimately be used for sandalwood (*Santalum album*) – from *chandan* in Hindi to *kulavuri* in Tamil – and the chemistry varies hugely. The oil derives from a hemiparasitic tree that grows on the roots of other plants, mostly other trees. A tree does not start to produce the sandols that are the active ingredient until it is about 30–45 years old. So if someone plants a tree, it will be their children who will benefit from it.

India accounts for 90 per cent of world supplies of sandalwood oil, but production is declining because the trees are becoming harder to find. 'In India there was a lot of pilfering of trees going on because the wood is used in many different ways, and there wasn't enough to meet the trade demand,' explains Monique. 'Sandalwood is an expensive essential oil. We wanted to know more about issues in the trade because we knew that there weren't enough supplies and that there was underhand activity going on. We examined oil from 30 or so suppliers and didn't find a single one selling sandalwood at the quality required by international standards. We also found that some were selling synthetic sandalwood as a natural extract. When we went back to the suppliers and asked if they had evidence that their sandalwood came from sustainable supplies, some started to get worried.'

ABOVE: Fragrant sandalwood oil is used in skin and hair products.

Developing local knowledge

Sustainability now lies at the heart of Kew's work with medicinal plants. In Africa it is working with a non-governmental organization called Garden Africa to try to establish 1001 community gardens over the next five years. The project aims to take existing knowledge of local plants and use this to help communities build gardens for growing crops and medicinal plants in a sustainable way. Kew is assisting by offering its expertise in propagating plants and providing scientific evidence on which species have medicinal uses. In particular, it is helping with a project to create a community garden on a 10-hectare (25-acre) plot at the Africulture Centre in Grahamstown, South Africa. Funded by the UK Department for Environment, Food & Rural Affairs (Defra), this garden will be a training ground exhibiting different types of plants and gardens, with a centre where it can sell plants or plant-based products, such as soaps, to raise money. Rhodes University Botanical Garden has already agreed to buy its indigenous plants from the garden.

'What is so great about this project is that it is not just about people coming in and saying we should do this or that. It's about developing the knowledge that's there,' says Monique. 'We're saying: "These are your plants and your practices, but if need be, we at Kew can help with methods of propagating the plants or comparing the activity of potential medicinal plants." We can say that one species is slightly better than another because we have carried out scientific tests. Or we can advise people that they shouldn't use a particular plant too much because we know it can accumulate in the body and cause renal failure. It's not about giving aid money; it's about helping communities at grass roots level.'

In 2006 Kew helped raise the profile of the project by supporting Garden Africa's entry at the Chelsea Flower Show. Set up in the same way as one of the community gardens in Africa, the exhibit's focus was a spiral of African crops and medicinal species. These were interspersed with plants known to be pest deterrents. The spiral radiated out from a shade tree, which in Africa might be a fever tree, an acacia karroo, a yellow wood or an African olive. 'Planting in long lines maximizes the crop yield, but allows "wash-out", which is when heavy rains wash bare soils away,' explains Monique. 'But if you have a small garden that is supporting a family or a few families, spiral planting is an effective way to avoid that.'

The gardeners also used a mulch of grasses, leaves and straw to prevent wash-out, which came in useful when heavy rains afflicted the Chelsea show. The garden was deliberately planted on a slope, with water-loving plants at the bottom and more drought-tolerant ones towards the top, as this is a good way of using water efficiently.

In the top left-hand corner stood a homestead, fashioned using recycled items and customized with township mural art. Built with the prevailing wind direction in mind, it provided protection for the 'family' and 'working' areas of the garden used to

OPPOSITE: Garden Africa's design for the Chelsea Flower Show in 2006 incorporated useful food and medicinal plants.

Rainforest plants are important contributors to Western medicine. So far researchers have scrutinized only 1 per cent of the plants that grow in rainforests, so it's possible that cures for currently incurable diseases, such as AIDS and cancer, could be found there. However, with scientists predicting that climate change will cause many plants to become extinct, we are in danger of losing medicinal plants before we have even begun to discover their benefits. Below are just a few of the plants grown at Kew that have been proven in recent years to have valuable medicinal uses.

Madagascar periwinkle (*Catharanthus roseus*)

Crops of the Madagascar periwinkle are grown in Tanzania and Texas to provide the anti-cancer drugs vincristine and vinblastine. These injectable drugs and their derivatives, such as vinorelbine, interfere with the division of cancer cells. They improve the chances of survival for a child with leukaemia from 20 per cent to 75 per cent. A recent laboratory study showed that chemicals in the plant may also prevent the growth of new blood vessels that support tumour growth. This plant is now extinct in the wild.

Pacific yew tree (*Taxus brevifolia*)

During the 1960s research workers in North Carolina, USA, isolated a crude extract from yew bark that was effective against human tumours. It took many years to find a way of obtaining sufficient quantities of the drug in a renewable way but eventually, in the 1990s, Taxol became an important treatment for ovarian and breast cancer. As insufficient amounts of the active ingredient could be extracted from Pacific yew, it is manufactured from clippings of common yew hedges, which are collected and sent to France for processing.

Yam (*Dioscorea mexicana*)

Steroids present in extracts of the yam were once modified to produce oestrogen, which is used in the birth control pills taken by 80 million women a day. Today the hormone is made from soya beans.

Maidenhair tree (*Ginkgo biloba*)

As the maidenhair is the world's oldest living species of tree, it's not surprising that its seeds have been used medicinally for thousands of years, not least by the Chinese. It has been found to be effective in treating Alzheimer's disease and other types of dementia.

Daffodil (*Narcissus*) and Snowdrop (*Galanthus nivalis*)

Scientists have discovered that galanthamine, which occurs in both daffodils (see opposite) and snowdrop bulbs, can help alleviate progressive degeneration of the brain. However, 10 tonnes of daffodil bulbs are needed to produce 1 kilogram (2.2 pounds) of galanthamine.

prepare food and dry medicinal plants. Old tyres and crates provided steps up the slope to help prevent soil erosion, while oil drums made suitable compost bins. In the bottom left-hand corner were plants known to yield fertilizer, which included nettles, yarrow, common comfrey and lovage. A fence built from acacia karroo, which has strong, white thorns, enclosed the garden – in Africa, a necessary barrier against wandering animals.

'We weren't able to have every plant at Chelsea that would be available in Africa, but we did include the aloes and Plectanthus plants that we had been testing for their medicinal uses here at Kew,' Monique continues. 'The Plectanthus species we used were ones that were known to have been used traditionally to treat malaria, and when we carried out tests we found that, by golly, they worked.'

BELOW: Old tyres and spiral planting helped avoid 'wash-out' at the Chelsea Flower Show.

Chelsea's African garden is now a permanent educational exhibit at the Eden Project in Cornwall. In Africa around 30 training gardens have so far been developed in three different sub-Saharan countries. Each garden costs around £10,000, but the figure varies according to its location and other social and environmental considerations, such as community health, terrain, access to water and security. Once established, the hope is that the network of 1001 gardens will train up to 50,000 people a week, and over a five-year period will help to create more than 500,000 new family and community gardens. The underlying strategy is to boost nutrition, particularly in areas with high levels of HIV infection. Malnutrition increases people's susceptibility to HIV, and lowers the body's ability to fight the disease once a person is infected. The project also hopes to reverse the negative thinking that evolved during the apartheid era, when gardens were used as 'punishment areas' for children.

The overall aim is to promote gardens as tools for teaching about environmental issues, agriculture, nutrition and medicinal plants. 'We're trying to address the needs of local people in terms of nutrition, medicine and conservation,' says John Nzira, one of Garden Africa's trainers and an expert in urban farming. 'We train people whom we think will have some influence in their communities to set up gardens in the local school or clinic. The aim is that they will then pass the information on to individuals who can set up a garden in their own backyard.'

Multiple identities

One of the difficulties Kew encounters in working with communities around the world is the profusion of names assigned to each plant species. People often identify plants using local rather than Latin names, and there may be many different local names throughout a country. Kew is hoping to reduce confusion through a project it is working on with the World Health Organization. The idea is to build up a database listing plants under their Latin names, then link these to various agreed taxonomic names and to all the different common names, together with the locations those names relate to. In the long term, Monique hopes it will become a global-scale reference tool, but her team is initially concentrating on African plants because so many people on the continent rely on them for medicine. Over time, she plans to make more of Kew's information resources available on the web so that researchers in Africa and other countries can have direct access to them.

'If you look at the information we have at Kew on African plants, it's more extensive than what's available in African libraries,' she says. 'If you go to a herbarium in a country such as Ghana, you have books from the 1930s, 1940s and 1950s, but very little up-to-date information. Yet here at Kew we have reports written by British scientists who have visited Africa much more recently. The information resource at Kew is huge. It's basically our history, and we want to use it in ways that will benefit the people in the countries from which it came. That doesn't necessarily mean we should be handing back artefacts and samples that were gifted to Kew. We can't alter our heritage, but we can use it in a constructive way.'

FIGHTING CRIME

ONE OF THE MORE UNUSUAL ROLES carried out by Kew staff is that of sleuth. If archaeologists want to find out what wood an artefact is made from, or customs officers need to know if a consignment of plants contains threatened species, there is usually someone at the gardens who can help. Identifying whole plants is a job for the Herbarium experts, but if material is broken up this calls for some clever detective work from scientists in the Jodrell Laboratory. In recent years they have identified a rope from ancient Egypt as being made from papyrus and recognized woody cabbage stems in a tin of soup. Occasionally, Kew is consulted about major crimes where plant remains, such as pollen or grass seeds, have been left at the scene of a robbery or murder. 'Forensic labs are not that well set up for botanical inquiries, so if there's fragmentary plant material involved, it will often come to us,' explains Peter Gasson, a plant anatomist based at the Jodrell Laboratory.

A high-profile case

One particularly disturbing case that Kew is helping investigate is that involving the headless torso of a young boy found in the river Thames in London in 2001. An autopsy indicated that the child's limbs had been severed very skilfully, his throat slit and his body drained of blood. This led the police to think that Adam, as they named him, might have been killed in a ritual sacrifice. With no fingerprints or dental records to help identify the boy, the police turned to forensic evidence for leads. Trace minerals absorbed from food and water vary according to which part of the world people live in, so forensic scientists began by analysing the levels of these minerals in Adam's bones. They discovered that the amounts of strontium, copper and lead present were two and a half times higher than would normally be expected in a child living in England. 'The police found there was a very great similarity between Adam's bones and those in cemeteries in Benin, Nigeria, so they concluded he came from that area,' says honorary research fellow Hazel Wilkinson, a retired plant anatomist and Kew's answer to the fictional sleuth Miss Marple.

The police Forensic Science Service sent Kew some highly magnified black-and-white images of material found in the boy's gut to see if they could identify what he had eaten. These images appeared to show clay pellets, quartz grains, small particles of gold, fragments of ground-down bone, plus four or five plant remains. Staff in the Jodrell Laboratory, the Herbarium and at Wakehurst Place initially felt unable to identify the remains, but then an unusual coincidence prompted Hazel to think it might be possible. 'I reckoned that whoever carried out the sacrifice might have given the boy some plants that would have knocked him out so he wouldn't struggle,' she recalls. 'If you look at the plant material in the pictures, you can see long, I-shaped sclereids – cells with very thick walls – and you find things like that in certain groups of Leguminosae that grow in the tropics. It so happened that a colleague of mine put an article up on the notice-board about the calabar bean, which belongs to this family. I thought it well worth investigating the structure of the bean because it grows in Nigeria and has a powerful sedative effect that could have paralysed or semi-paralysed the poor boy.'

Hazel asked around at the gardens to see if anyone had any specimens of calabar beans, and located a box of the large black seeds in the Museum of Economic Botany archives. She took one of the beans and ground it down with a pestle and mortar, trying to imitate what someone preparing a plant-based concoction might do. When she cut various thin sections and examined the fragments under a microscope, they looked very similar to the ones in the police images. And when she researched the uses of the calabar bean she discovered that witch doctors in Nigeria had traditionally used potions made from the plant in black magic rituals. Although human sacrifices were unusual, animal-blood offerings were frequently made in West African voodoo culture to communicate with the spirit world and gain protection from ancestral deities. So it was quite possible that Adam's last meal was a poisonous tincture composed, at least partially, of calabar beans.

When the significance of Hazel's findings was reported in the national press, the police brought her more material from Adam's lower intestine to see if she could identify any other plants. The specimen comprised a stringy mass of brown, rather flocculent (fluffy), foul-smelling liquid. On close examination, Hazel found it contained a variety of plant fragments, including a whole leaf, bits of hard-shelled seeds similar to those of the poisonous herb *Datura* (angel's trumpet), a hairy, sepal-like structure with recognizable oil glands, and some animal tissue. The police investigation had by now concluded that the boy probably came from the Yoruba tribe, one of the three largest ethnic groups in Nigeria. This prompted Hazel to consult a book written by Pierre Fatumbi Verger called *Ewé [Leaf]: The Use of Plants in Yoruba Society*, which listed many Nigerian plants and their medicinal applications. The author, who died only recently, had been initiated into the Yoruba religion Candomblé as a *babalâo* or 'father of secrets', and therefore understood the role plants played in religious rituals. Hazel thought if she could find a recipe giving the ingredients of concoctions used in ritual sacrifices, she would have some strong leads that could be useful in trying to identify the species represented by the fragments taken from Adam's stomach.

BELOW: Plants have long been used in African dances and rituals.

The book did indeed have a section called 'Death', but instead of listing ingredients that might cause it, the text merely said: 'We have nine formulae to kill people, which we are not going to give, but we are giving one of the 12 formulae that protect against death.' Hazel now hopes to obtain a copy of the death formulae. 'If it were possible to obtain the names of plants used in the formulae to kill people,' she says, 'that would be a much more direct route to potentially identifying the fragments from Adam's stomach. I could then go to the Herbarium, get some leaves and seeds from the relevant species, grind them up and compare them under the microscope to the material provided by the police.'

In the meantime, the police are still searching for the people who sacrificed the boy, but have jailed the ringleader of a gang they believe may have been involved in trafficking children specifically for sacrifice rituals. Hazel remains hopeful that her work may yet help lead the police to Adam's killers.

IN KEW'S ARCHIVES: **Calabar Beans**

High on a shelf in Kew's Economic Botany Archive is a small box of fat, black beans (see below). A handwritten note in faded ink attributes them to Dr T.J. Hutchinson, a medical officer in Old Calabar (in the then British Protectorate of Southern Nigeria), who served as a surgeon on the 1854 expedition to explore the Niger. He was British consul for the Bight of Biafra and the island of Fernando Po, the latter being the place where the beans were gathered.

The plant that bears the calabar bean, in thick brown pods, is a woody African vine known as the ordeal tree (*Physostigma venenosum*). This name relates to the use of calabar beans as an 'ordeal poison' in African trials during the nineteenth century. Anyone accused of murder or witchcraft would be made to eat the beans as a means of determining their guilt or innocence. If they died, they were guilty; if the bean had a purging effect without killing, they were also guilty and sold into slavery; if they vomited up the poison and survived, they were innocent.

Hutchinson quotes a local person on the outcome of eating the calabar bean: '"Him do dis," said one of the Kalabar gentlemen, describing to me its effects; and in the words, as well as the action suited to them, there was a graphic power impossible for me to transfer to paper – "Soap come out of him mout, and all him body walk" – a most perfect description of the frothing from the mouth, and the convulsive energy of the whole frame.'

Two cases of poisoning by calabar beans took place in Liverpool in 1864 and 1871. In both cases the sweepings from merchant marine vessels that had arrived from West African ports ended up on the dock. Children playing in the port found the beans and ate them, prompting them to be violently sick. Thanks to rapid medical attention, only one of 57 affected children died.

All this information proved very useful to Hazel Wilkinson at the Jodrell Laboratory when she was helping to solve a ritual killing (see page 69).

To catch a plant thief

It's not every day that Kew staff help apprehend child smugglers, but they are often asked to assist HM Revenue & Customs in preventing the trafficking of threatened wood and plants. According to the World Conservation Union, one in eight plants is threatened with extinction, and trade in some 25,000 species is now regulated under the Convention on International Trade in Endangered Species (CITES). CITES-listed species have Appendix I, II or III status, depending on how vulnerable they are. Appendix I bans commercial international trade; Appendix II requires a CITES permit for international trade, which is issued only if trading will not be detrimental to the survival of the species; and Appendix III-listed species can be traded subject to certain export conditions. Listed trees include *Fitzroya cupressoides*, one specimen of which in Chile was recorded to be 3622 years old; *Pterocarpus santalinus*, sometimes known as red sandalwood, the wood of which is prized for cabinetmaking;

and Brazilian mahogany, *Swietenia macrophylla*. Worldwide, 169 countries are signed up to the convention, which came into play in 1973. In Europe the 25 member states implement it through a series of trade regulations that are stricter than the basic CITES controls.

Each country signed up to CITES has a management authority that issues permits, and a scientific authority that advises on applications and conducts research into plant groups affected by trade. In the UK, Kew is the Scientific Authority for Plants for CITES. This means it is the first port of call when customs officers seize plants, or products made from plants, and need to identify the material. Between 2001 and 2005 Kew helped inspect 45,000 plants and over 62 tonnes of timber for HM Revenue & Customs, as well as training staff in basic plant identification. 'We help them become familiar with the main CITES plant groups, distinguish

wild from propagated plants, and outline the species most likely to be traded illegally,' explains Noel McGough, head of Kew's Conventions and Policy Section. 'Before we train them they think orchids are nice, big, flowering, glossy things – which they are when you buy them – but when they're traded they look completely different, with just leaves and roots. So the first thing we do is explain that if a customs officer stops someone and finds a pile of grubby leaves and roots in their bag, they may have something quite interesting that could be material collected in the wild. Propagated plants, on the other hand, are clean and uniform.'

Customs staff faced just this scenario in 2004, when pharmaceutical researcher Dr Sian Tiong Lim, travelling from Malaysia, came through Heathrow airport with more than 100 rare Asian slipper orchids in his luggage. The officials suspected the plants might be wild specimens, so called on Kew for assistance. Experts in the Herbarium soon realized that 126 of the 130 plants were of the genus *Paphiopedilum*. As this is listed under CITES Appendix I, all international trade is banned. Six of the plants proved to be *P. rothschildianum*, which is on the brink of extinction and restricted to the island of Borneo. Another specimen was *P. sandrianum*, which has drooping petals that grow to over 1 metre (3 feet) long. First spotted in 1885 and rediscovered in 1978, it now grows only in small numbers on remote, shady limestone cliffs in a national park in Sarawak, Borneo.

One of the rarest specimens in the haul was *P. gigantifolium*. This has broad, glossy leaves and grows only in river gorges on the Indonesian island of Sulawesi. Although discovered as recently as 1997, it may already be extinct in the wild because of illegal collection. Even Kew's orchid expert, Dave Roberts, had never seen one. 'Lim was stopped by customs staff when he was coming in from Malaysia, and as the material didn't match what he had permits for, they brought the plants here for identification,' recalls Noel. 'We realized that 126 were CITES Appendix I species that were native to a range of countries and were very rare.' Lim eventually pleaded guilty and was sentenced to four months in prison in early 2006. On behalf of HM Revenue & Customs, Kew is currently contacting some of the countries from which the plants were taken in order to coordinate their return and promote conservation of the species. 'Before we return any we have to be sure that they are free from infection, so they are now in strict quarantine,' Noel continues. 'The potential for bugs is quite high because the plants came from several countries and were mixed in transit, so we have to be very careful.'

One of the largest seizures involving Kew was a 26-tonne consignment of window blinds made from wood declared as non-CITES listed. A sharp-eyed customs official at Felixstowe container port suspected the blinds might be ramin, a light-coloured tropical hardwood that comes from several species of the tree *Gonystylus*, native to the peat swamp forests of Southeast Asia and the South Pacific. Being fine-grained and easy to work, ramin is often made into pool cues, tool handles and decorative mouldings. However, concern about its overexploitation, particularly within prime orang-utan habitats and protected reserves in Southeast Asia, led it to be listed under

BELOW:
Indiscriminate logging has left once lush forests bare and lifeless.

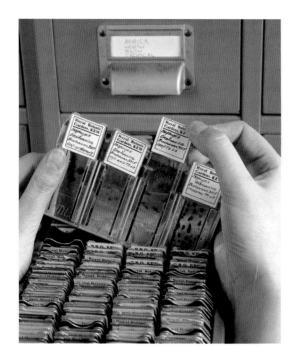

Appendix III of CITES in 2001. It has since been uplisted to Appendix II. This means it can now be traded only with the correct CITES export permits and European Union import permits.

'The blinds seized at Felixstowe were all painted or stained different colours,' explains Lydia White, a plant anatomist working with Peter Gasson in the Jodrell Laboratory. 'We have considerable experience of identifying ramin with a microscope, and can even recognize the end grain with a hand lens because the pattern of cells is very distinctive. We sliced the surface with a razor blade, inspected each of the slats, and realized that the blinds were made of a mixture of softwoods and hardwoods, including ramin. As a result, the shipment was confiscated.'

The Micromorphology Laboratory, at the end of a long corridor on the first floor of the Jodrell Laboratory, is crammed with tools that enable Kew's plant anatomists to identify virtually any wood from a specimen the size of a sugar cube. They boil the wood, then use a machine that looks like a small bacon slicer to create flakes of timber 25 micrometres thick, thinner than most human hairs. These slivers are placed on glass slides for inspection under a microscope. The cellular structure of the wood, including annual growth rings, produces characteristic grain patterns according to the species. These appear differently, depending on which plane the timber is cut along, so the scientists prepare three sections: one transverse, one tangential and one radial.

Along one wall of the laboratory six filing cabinets hold 100,000 slides arranged according to species, which the team use to compare their mystery samples against. The collection ranges from sections of wood brought back from India by famous nineteenth-century botanist and forester James Sykes Gamble, to slides of CITES-listed timbers recently prepared by Lydia or a Kew student. If there is no sample of the required wood in the filing cabinet, the scientists consult Kew's Economic Botany Archive to see if they have a piece from which a slide could be made, or they seek guidance from books such as *The Anatomy of the Dicotyledons* and *A Guide to Useful Woods of the World* that line the lab walls.

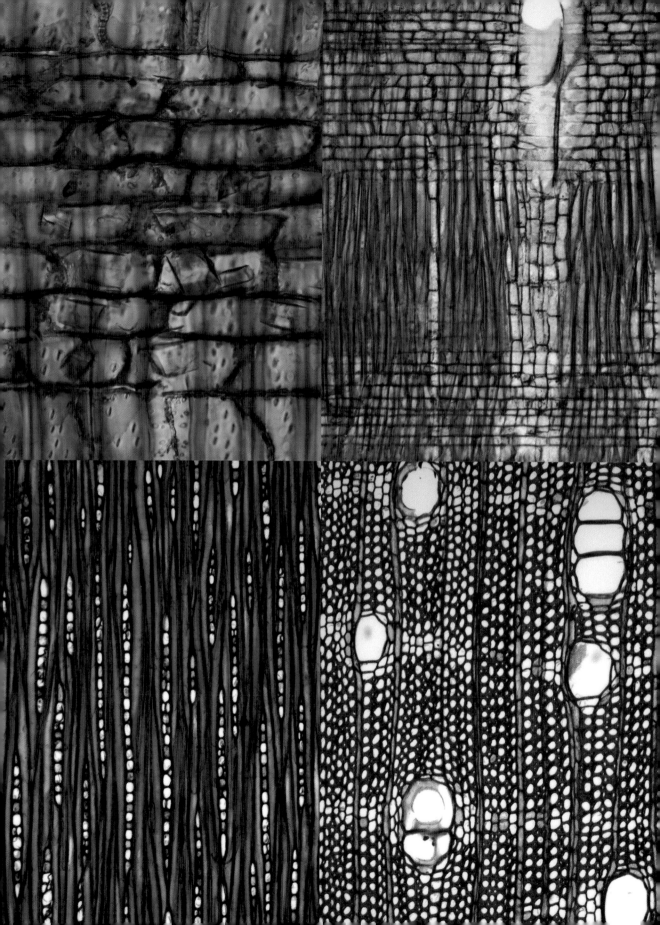

SEIZED WOOD PUT TO GOOD USE

Rather than allowing seized material to go back into trade, HM Revenue & Customs often donates material for educational or conservation uses. The visitor centre (see right) and schoolhouse at Wakehurst Place are both partially made of confiscated wood. The end walls of the former were built from a seizure of afrormosia (*Pericopsis elata*) that arrived in the UK from Zaire without the required export documents, while the latter was constructed using *Fitzroya cupressoides*, a softwood from South America.

'It's fitting that we can teach about conservation by telling children the story of where the wood came from while they're sitting in a building made from it,' says Noel McGough, head of Kew's Conventions and Policy Section.

'This book,' explains Peter, taking down one well-thumbed black-and-white volume, 'is an illustrated glossary of the anatomical characters we use when we're identifying hardwoods. In case you don't know, hardwoods are all dicotyledons [flowering plants whose seeds typically contain two embryonic leaves or cotyledons], and softwoods are gymnosperms, mostly conifers, which are vascular plants whose seeds are not enclosed by fruit. It's quite confusing that there are some very soft hardwoods; for example, balsa is a hardwood, but it is a lot softer than most softwoods.' Actually identifying the species is a case of recognizing subtle differences in a species' tissue structure. 'If you look at a transverse section, you have about four major cell types,' he continues. 'First there are the vessels, essentially the plumbing that transports water up the tree. Then you have fibres, which are thick-walled cells that support the tree and give it its strength. There are also thin-walled cells called "axial parenchyma", and finally you have "rays", which are like the spokes in a wheel. All four of these cell types can vary in just about any way you can imagine. For example, the vessels or pores can be solitary, small or large, in pairs or clusters, and so on. And the parenchyma cells, which store starch, come in all sorts of patterns with obscure names. But essentially it's the variations of these four characteristics that make oak wood look like oak, beech wood look like beech, and so on.'

Identifying ancient materials

Requests for assistance from customs officials often require Kew just to confirm that a wood is of a particular type, such as in the case of the ramin blinds. But sometimes Peter receives requests from antiques dealers, furniture importers or members of the public asking for help in identifying and finding the provenance of an unknown species of wood from scratch. This can be quite difficult – for example, it took Peter two days to identify a sample of *Berchemia zeyheri*, or 'pink ivory', one of the world's most valuable woods, from South Africa.

On another occasion a request from Sir David Attenborough for help in identifying the wood of an antique statue he had bought on Easter Island required some clever detective work from Paula Rudall, head of micromorphology. Easter Island no longer has any trees on it because its ancient inhabitants cut them all down. The mystery timber turned out to be the hardwood *Sophora toromiro*. This tree is now extinct in the wild, but a handful remain growing in a selection of European botanical gardens. Kew did not have any samples of the wood, but it did have specimens from two closely related species from South America and New Zealand. An example of one of these, *Sophora microphylla*, was felled to make way for the extension to the Jodrell Laboratory.

BELOW: The branches of *Sophora microphylla*.

'We often get requests to identify unusual woods because our remit is to identify anything from anywhere,' says Peter. 'But that's a bit of a tall order really. I have a piece of a walking stick here that someone has sent in, and at the moment I haven't the foggiest idea what it's made of.'

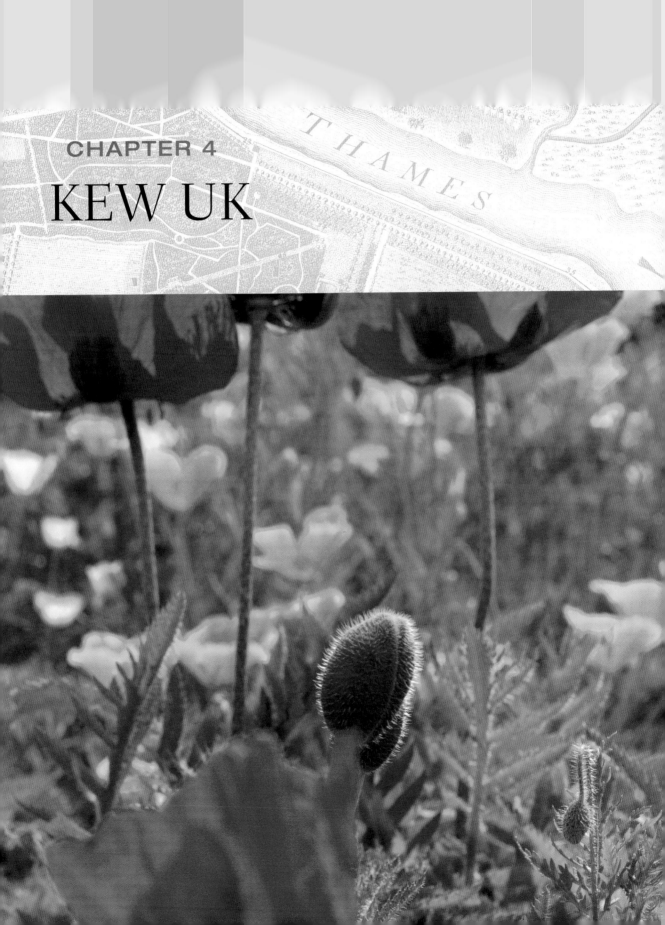

CHAPTER 4

KEW UK

WE OFTEN HEAR WARNINGS in the media about the destruction of the world's tropical rainforests and coral reefs, but there is less coverage of the plight of Britain's flora. At the start of the millennium Kew helped develop the Global Strategy for Plant Conservation. This framework links disparate plant conservation initiatives and outlines targets to be met by 2010, including goals for conserving the UK's 1450 species. The aim is for 60 per cent of the country's threatened plants to be conserved by the year 2010. So far progress has been slow: in 2006 Kew, Plantlife International and the Joint Nature Conservation Committee warned that only 20 per cent of threatened flowering plant species were currently recognized as priorities for conservation. 'We are finding it a challenge to meet these ambitious targets, even here in the UK with a relatively small and well-documented flora,' said Kew's then director Sir Peter Crane. 'This makes us all the more aware of the greater challenge faced by our counterparts in tropical countries with far greater plant diversity and much more limited resources.'

Millennium Seed Bank

As you would expect, Kew is at the forefront of efforts to conserve Britain's plants. The initial goal of the Millennium Seed Bank at Wakehurst Place was to store seeds from the entire British flora. It has now achieved that, apart from a few elusive species. 'We've got 96 per cent,' says Steve Alton, UK coordinator in the seed bank's Conservation Department. 'Of the remaining 4 per cent, some of those are things that can't be banked, such as our two native oak species, the sessile oak (*Quercus petraea*) and the pedunculate or English oak (*Quercus robur*). They can't be stored because, like 15 per cent of the world's flora, their seeds won't tolerate being dried.'

Other tricky customers include a plant called the yellow star of Bethlehem. 'It's not so rare that people know exactly where it is, and it's not so common that you can just go out and find it. It's small and flowers in March, when people aren't usually looking, and by the time seeds are produced, the vegetation has grown really tall, so

you can't see it. Added to that, slugs like it, so if you do find it, there's a good chance that the seed pods will have been eaten. The plant's got everything going wrong for it, but we will get it eventually.'

The value of storing seeds is evident when you visit the Micropropagation Laboratory at Kew. Tucked away behind Climbers and Creepers on the western edge of the gardens, this is where staff such as Grace Prendergast and Jenny Rowntree spend hours coaxing stubborn seeds into life in the hope of saving their species from the brink of extinction. In chilled rooms, row upon row of jars contain these premature babies of the plant world. Sometimes it takes the staff years to work out what conditions are required to make a seed turn into a plant, but once they've cracked it, the potential for success is great. For example, what was the only remaining lady's slipper orchid (*Cypripedium calceolus*) in the UK, a single plant in the north of England, has now been supplemented by 80 of Kew's home-grown seedlings. 'There's a warden who looks after the remaining plant in the wild and pollinates it by hand, taking the pollen and putting it on the stigma,' explains Grace, scientific officer on the Sainsbury Orchid Conservation Project. 'In some years it's had up to 15 flowers on it, so he's collected the seed pods and sent them to us at Kew.'

From seed to plant

Gathering seeds is one thing, but turning them into healthy plants is another. For a start, the time at which they are gathered can be critical. When Grace first began trying to germinate seeds from the lady's slipper orchid she had no success at all. Then an orchid specialist in Canada got in touch to say he had been able to propagate another *Cypripedium* species using immature seeds. 'Although the plant they were trying to germinate was a rare species in Canada, there were around 100 plants rather than just one, and they were able to conduct pollinations and collect the seed pods at different times to find out the best time to gather them,' says Grace. 'That turned out to be about 50 days after pollination, so we tried it here and it worked with the British one as well.'

The ingredients of the growing media, agar – essentially a jelly-like cocktail of nutrients designed to give the plant the best possible start in life – is also important. Grace tried out a lot of well-known growing media without success before a Swedish amateur orchid grower contacted her with a recipe he had been successfully using to germinate a variety of European orchid. 'He's a paediatrician by trade, and the concoction he created has pineapple juice in it, along with special vitamins and amino acids that are designed for premature babies,' she says. 'Once we had that medium, and knowing we needed to use the immature seeds, we started to get almost 100 per cent germination. As one seed pod can contain thousands of seeds, that meant we could grow large numbers of plants.'

Grace now grows several hundred of the orchids a year, 500 of which go to the sponsors, English Nature, and the rest to bolster Kew's collections. Germination takes one or two months, during which time the spherical seed embryos atop the nutrient jelly in the Petri dishes swell up and burst out of their seed coats to form 'protocorms' 2 millimetres (⅛ inch) long. After that a shoot starts to develop, followed by two or three roots. At this stage, a few months after sowing, the plantlets are moved into larger containers (actually old honey jars). The roots keep on growing and resemble spaghetti. Just over a year after sowing, the plantlets are taken out of the agar jelly, washed with sterile water and then put into sealed plastic bags in the fridge for the winter. When spring comes around, they're potted up. The ones designated for reintroduction are kept for a few more years until they're deemed big enough to survive, and then they are planted out.

As well as the lab-reared plants that have been reintroduced close to the one remaining wild plant, others have been put in places where it used to grow. Kew's researchers know the whereabouts of the lady's slipper orchids' former strongholds because there are lots of Herbarium specimens with notes saying where their voracious collectors picked them. The Victorians liked the flower's attractive yellow pouch and deep red sepals, so they tried to grow them in their gardens. However, the orchid is very particular about its growing conditions, so many died. 'In Britain they grow only on open chalk grassland, but, strangely, in the rest of Europe they are usually found in pine woods,' says Grace. There's also one in Kew's Rock Garden, near the School of Horticulture and the Order Beds.

Having now propagated some 8000 of the lady's slipper orchids, Grace has her eye on the UK's other species. There are 49 orchids native to the UK, including some relatively common ones, such as spotted orchids (*Dactylorhiza*), bee orchids (*Ophrys*) and fragrant orchids (*Gymnadenia*), and some very rare ones. The World Conservation Union's British Red Data List cites the lady's slipper, the red helliborine, the ghost orchid and the sub-species *ochroleuca* of the early marsh orchid as critically endangered. A further seven species and subspecies are considered to be endangered or vulnerable. Some of Kew's core funding is designated to propagating rare orchids, and Grace has already carried out experiments to discover the best ways of sparking germination for

the other most threatened species. 'We know how to germinate most of them, but we will need to grow them in large numbers for a reintroduction programme and that will take a lot of time,' she says. 'It's a case of prioritizing what to do first.'

The tale of the UK's fiftieth orchid species, the summer lady's tresses (*Spiranthes aestivalis*), is a lingering reminder of why Kew's propagating skills are invaluable. First recorded in 1840 growing among sphagnum bogs in the New Forest in Hampshire, the last-known photograph of it was taken in July 1937. The draining of its prime habitat, and collecting, both contributed to its becoming extinct.

Saving the Cinderellas

It's not only the showy, overcollected flowering plants that Kew is trying to conserve, however. It is also running a programme investigating the possibility of reintroducing rare British bryophytes, the collective name given to mosses, liverworts and hornworts. Bryophytes grow in almost all terrestrial habitats, including rainforests, Arctic ecosystems and deserts, where they help regulate ecosystem processes, such as nutrient, water and carbon recycling. Many species grow in the UK and Ireland, but several are threatened with decline or extinction. Jenny Rowntree, Kew's bryophyte conservation officer, is conducting experiments to find ways of growing and storing bryophytes, with the aim of reintroducing some to sites around the UK. 'A lot of the conservation activities that go on in Britain are governed by UK Biodiversity Action Plans, of which there are two types – habitat and species plans,' she explains. 'I work with those bryophytes that have Biodiversity Action Plans. Written into some of those plans is the requirement to grow the plants "off site" – that is, outside their natural environment – and to keep them in a collection. So that's what I do.'

Jenny grows bryophytes in what is termed 'axenic culture'. This means it is free from fungi, algae or bacteria. Although this is very different from the natural environment in which the plants grow, it provides a reliable method for propagating them. In order to grow in axenic cultures, the plants must first be cleaned in a mild solution of bleach to remove contaminants. Jenny has mastered methods for cultivating bryophytes using tissue taken from fruiting bodies and leaf shoots. Like Grace, she grows her charges on a layer of jelly, but the levels of nutrients are much lower than those used for orchids. Jenny maintains a 'living collection' of her plants in a small incubator at the Micropropagation Laboratory. Stored in Petri dishes, the samples all look rather small, green and mossy to the uninitiated, but Jenny can distinguish many different species among them. 'I've got 24 or 25 species in the living collection, and about 15 of those are also stored in liquid nitrogen as part of a "cryopreserved" or frozen collection,' she explains. 'I'm trying to freeze everything I have in the living collection as a back-up.'

Plants undergoing cryopreservation are placed in tiny vials in tall canisters at very low temperatures (-196°C/-320°F), which keeps them alive, but in suspended animation so that they don't grow at all. It is useful to store many plants in this way because when they are continually 'subcultured', as is required to maintain a living

BELOW: *Dicranum scoparium*, a bryophyte moss.

collection, they can sometimes become adapted to the sterile laboratory conditions. This is a problem if your aim is to reintroduce species to the outside world, but the chances of adaptations taking place are lessened if plants are stored frozen. Jenny has now managed to hone her preservation methods and now successfully stores both living and frozen bryophytes. She is currently experimenting with growing large numbers of one species, the slender thread-moss (*Orthodontium gracile*), with a view to reintroducing it to the unique sandstone rock habitat in Wakehurst's Francis Rose Reserve, a Site of Special Scientific Interest. 'I've been trying to develop methods of taking things out of the freezer and growing them so that they can survive outside and then be put back into a semi-natural environment,' she says.

The fruits of her efforts are lined up along the outside of Aiton House in which the Micropropagation Laboratory is located. Beside the access route that leads past the main entrance are three frames 2 metres (6 feet) long covered by a green mesh to keep the sun off. Beneath it are around 150 plants growing on individual plugs of rock, each placed in an open-top glass jar. 'First I grew them in the lab for 12 weeks in sterile conditions,' explains Jenny. 'Then I took them out of the lab, removed the lids from the jars and placed them outside.' The idea of this was slowly to initiate the fragile bryophytes into the polluted, bacteria-rich outside world. Eventually, when the rocks are showing a healthy covering of green growth, they will be taken on their rock hosts and placed in holes excavated in the sandstone at Wakehurst Place. 'If they can grow here at Kew, they should be able to grow there,' Jenny says.

Commercial pressures

One of the pressures on bryophytes growing in the wild comes from the floristry and horticulture trades, where mosses such as heath plait moss (*Hypnum jutlandicum*) and glittering wood moss (*Hyclocomium splendens*) are harvested to provide colour and add texture to flower arrangements, and to line hanging baskets. The lichen *Cladonia potentosa* is also collected. This may be used for making trees for model railways, as the closely related species *Cladonia stellaris* is imported for this purpose. Much gathered bryophyte material comes from land owned by the Forestry Commission in Wales. In the report *Britain's Wild Harvest*, published by Kew in 2004, authors Hew Prendergast and Helen Sanderson reported that as many as

IN KEW'S ARCHIVES: **Products made from British plants**

A recent addition to Kew's Economic Botany Archive is a collection of items derived from British plants. A surprisingly large number of products are made using plants collected in the wild in Britain, although many of the industries are necessarily small scale. Seaweed, elder, nettles, willow bark, marsh samphire and a variety of mosses are all gathered and processed for sale in products such as cordials, soaps (see below left), skin products, tinctures and fertilizers.

The soothing and anti-bacterial properties of many British plants make them especially suitable as ingredients in skincare products. One Kent-based company uses nettles, elder, roses, comfrey, alder and beech in its luxury soaps, while a Scottish-based company harvests red and green seaweed species from the remote rocky islets around Mull. Rich in iron and calcium respectively, the seaweeds are used to make a variety of lotions and creams for 2000 shops around the world.

Of the 300 professional basket-makers in the UK, over 80 collect their raw ingredients from hedgerows and woods to supplement imported materials, such as bamboo and rattan. The most important British plant used in this traditional craft industry is willow (see below right). The willow trees growing in large numbers on the waterlogged Somerset Levels once supported a thriving basket-making industry, but this went into decline when modern materials made the trade unviable. Today the region is seeing a revival of the old basket-making methods, and the willows are being harvested once more.

50 articulated lorries were filled with moss annually by just one company. Although the collecting activities are regulated by a licence system, they found that illicit collectors were targeting certain sites. In July 1993 the first conviction under the Wildlife and Countryside Act 1981 took place for the unauthorized collection of 26 large sacks of moss. The authors concluded that information on which species were targeted, the total amounts gathered and the timescales of regrowth was severely lacking. However, they also reported that one collector believes there could be a huge market for non-timber forest products that could benefit the health of woodlands if managed in a sustainable way.

The report threw up interesting findings about other wild plants that are harvested on a small scale across the UK. Wild elder, which has a long history of use in traditional medicine, is being increasingly gathered for use in cordials. Indeed, three well-known companies are using wild elder flowers and fruit in a commercially viable way. Each May and June, one of these companies, which sells over a million bottles of cordial a year, employs 600 people to scour the hedgerows and pick the elder flowers, sourcing half of its raw material in this way. Since demand is increasing, some individual suppliers and companies are experimenting with cultivating elder, the first time this has been tried in Britain. Early results show that plantation bushes can produce a harvestable crop of flowers, although the plants are susceptible to damage from insects.

Another successful cottage industry is making use of the club rush (*Schoenoplectus lacustris*), which commonly grows in the waters of lowland Britain. One company gathers rushes primarily from the Great Ouse River that runs through Bedfordshire and Cambridgeshire. The harvesters use flat-bottomed, aluminium punts to wend their way through the reeds, slicing off great bundles with scythes as they go. The stems are tied together into 'bolts' for weaving or plaiting into mats, baskets, chair seats, bags and a host of other items. The company uses 20 per cent of the 90-tonne wet harvest it gathers between June and August, and sells a further 20 per cent on to other weavers. The remainder is sold to Scottish whisky manufacturers, who insert strips of club rush between oak panels on whisky casks to act as a sealant. They have found the longer British rushes to be of better quality than the Dutch species they have occasionally used. The rushes yield a good price and are not a cause for concern in terms of conservation because the company harvests sites only once every three years.

Alcoholic drinks derived from plants are being increasingly made in Britain. Aside from grapes and hops, the source ingredients include birch sap, heather, rowan berries, sloe berries and blackberries. One company, based near Strathaven in Scotland, specializes in beers based on wild plants. Its most famous product is Fraoch heather ale, which is flavoured with heather flowers and bog myrtle leaves. It also uses bladderwrack (*Fucus vesiculosus*) to brew kelpie seaweed ale.

At the other end of Britain, the south of England is becoming popular as a wine-growing region, with vineyards now thriving in Surrey, Gloucestershire, Sussex, Kent and Cornwall. While the grapes used are generally from planted vineyards, some wild plants are used to flavour the wines. A winery in Petworth, West Sussex, uses the grapes from five local vineyards, together with naturally harvested products, such as birch bark taken from trees growing in its grounds. Some industry experts have suggested that Britain's wine-making potential is increasing because of warmer temperatures caused by global warming.

BELOW: Club rushes, *Schoenoplectus lacustris*, harvested on the Great Ouse River from a flat-bottomed punt.

All change?

Kew monitors the British weather using the centuries-old technique of phenology. This involves recording natural events in nature, such as the times at which plants flower or hibernating animals appear. Over a long period of time, figures can be scrutinized to see if any trends emerge. Phenology has been undertaken at Kew for the past 50 years, largely thanks to Nigel Hepper. A former Herbarium botanist, Nigel came through the same entrance to the gardens every day and recorded plants on the way to his office and again at lunch time. When he retired, Kew continued to record information on 100 of the plants he monitored. These are now known as the Kew 100. The information gathered is fed to the National Phenology Network, which has non-continuous plant records going back to the 1640s.

Although 50 years is not a particularly long time, Kew has already spotted an emerging trend in its records. 'The flowering times of many cultivated plants vary a lot from year to year, depending on the weather in the run-up to flowering,' explains Sandra Bell, wildlife and environment recording coordinator. 'That's particularly the case with spring-flowering plants; they can be weeks early or weeks late either side of their average. However, over the 50 years that Nigel has been recording at Kew there is a discernible trend towards earlier flowering in many species. That would seem to be a fairly clear indication that those plants have responded to a change in the overall average temperatures.' It may be no coincidence that on 10 August 2003 a temperature of 38.1°C (100.6°F) was recorded at Kew, which is considered by many to be the highest temperature ever recorded in the UK.

BELOW: The varying dates on which plants such as daffodils begin to bloom each year help scientists monitor changes to our weather. In 2006 the spring bloom came surprisingly late.

CHAPTER 5

PLANET KEW

PREVIOUS PAGE: King
proteas, *Protea
cynaroides*, grow
in the wild below
Table Mountain,
South Africa.

EVER SINCE PRINCESS AUGUSTA CREATED a physic garden at Kew to display exotic species, the gardens have had connections with foreign climes. During the eighteenth century Kew collectors, such as Francis Masson, Joseph Banks and Ernest Wilson, made perilous journeys all over the world to bring back seeds and specimens. If it weren't for their tenacity and dedication, we wouldn't today enjoy plants such as the striking orange and purple bird of paradise (*Strelitzia reginae*), the vivid crimson spikes of the bottlebrush plant (*Callistemon citrinus*) or the elegant and perfumed regal lily (*Lilium regale*) in our gardens.

As the British Empire expanded, Kew played an influential role in advising the government on which newly discovered plants could be economically useful. It set up botanical gardens in the colonies to help it to translocate plants, such as rubber, cinchona (the source of quinine), coffee, tea and breadfruit. As the resulting profitable plantations greatly benefited the empire, little thought was given at that time to the impact on the people and indigenous floras of the countries concerned.

With the global population now exceeding 6.5 billion, once richly diverse and healthy habitats are under intense pressure. Across the Amazon, western Africa and Southeast Asia, rainforests are being annihilated for their timber by uncontrolled and often illegal logging activities. In the tropics alone over 5 million square kilometres (2 million square miles) of forest have been degraded by destructive logging, and a further 3.5 million square kilometres (1.4 million square miles) totally deforested during the last few decades.

Changes in the global climate prompted by human activities are also putting pressure on plants, especially those living on the fringes of their favoured habitats. Scientists at Conservation International, a US-based non-profit organization, warn that if climate change predictions for 2050 come true, more than a quarter of all land animals and plants could face extinction. In developing countries, where large numbers of people rely on local plants for medicines and building materials, the impacts are likely to be devastating.

OPPOSITE: The
bottlebrush plant,
Callistemon citrinus,
was introduced to
Britain from Australia
in 1788 by Sir
Joseph Banks.

Global conservation and Kew

Faced with such gloomy predictions, Kew's prime motivation is now the conservation of the world's flora. At the start of the millennium it helped develop the Global Strategy for Plant Conservation, a framework that links disparate plant conservation initiatives and outlines targets to be met by 2010. The strategy is now incorporated into a plan for reducing biodiversity loss agreed by 122 environment ministers at the Eighth Conference of the Parties of the Convention on Biological Diversity held in Brazil in 2006. One hundred and fifty government leaders had signed up to the convention at the 1992 Rio Earth Summit. Its objectives are: 'The conservation of biological diversity, the sustainable use of its components, and the fair and equitable sharing of the benefits arising out of the utilization of genetic resources.'

Kew works with international partners, ranging from non-governmental organizations (NGOs) and charities to research institutions, commercial companies and governments. In recent years it has produced in-depth assessments of eight major habitats, and provided advice on how to conserve 3000 individual species. It provides specimens and field guides so that partners on the ground can identify plants and assess environmental change. If necessary, it also propagates rare species, saving them from extinction. The café marron (*Ramosmania rodriguesii*), an endemic plant from the island of Rodrigues in the Indian Ocean, was thought to be extinct in the wild until an observant schoolboy spotted a single surviving tree in 1980. Kew's horticultural staff managed to root cuttings and eventually worked out how to set fruit. The café marron bore its first fruit with viable seeds in 2003, and specimens have now been sent back to Rodrigues.

'Our work abroad involves everything from describing a single new species to helping countries deliver their plant conservation strategies,' explains Eimear Nic Lughadha, head of Science Operations at Kew. 'We might be working out if two closely related plants are two species or just one, challenging and testing theories put forward by Darwin, or developing new techniques in molecular identification.'

Several of the overseas campaigns at Kew are large-scale endeavours involving institutions across several continents. One such venture aims to explore and conserve 'hot spots' of biodiversity, where great concentrations of rare or unique species are found. Conservation International has identified around 34 such areas, based on the abundance of different plants and animals that exist there, the number of species found only at that location, and the threats facing the region. They include the Atlantic Forest of tropical South America, where 20,000 plant species thrive, but where 90 per cent of the forest has been destroyed; the California Floristic Province, which is home to the planet's largest living organism, the giant redwood tree (*Sequoiadendron giganteum*); and the coastal forests of East Africa, source of the 40,000 cultivated varieties of African violet that form the basis of a US$100 million global house-plant trade.

BELOW: Redwoods growing in the wild.

Gathering data and raising awareness

Of course, it's only possible to highlight areas rich in biodiversity if someone has been out and gathered information on the plants that exist there. In many parts of the world even simple data on native plants is lacking. One area where Kew has been working to improve knowledge of the flora is Cameroon in West Africa, where vast tropical rainforests teem with plants, animals and fungi found nowhere else on Earth. Kew's link with the country dates back to 1861, when the gardens' first director, Sir William Hooker, dispatched plant collector Gustav Mann to the Gulf of Guinea. The hardwood *Oncoba mannii* is one of many species from Africa in which his name is immortalized. Since Mann's early forays into Cameroon's forests, the Herbarium at Kew has built up an extensive reference collection of plants from the country, some 60,000 of which are now listed on a computer database. This material is now helping Cameroonian botanists to learn more about their country's flora.

BELOW: Collecting the seed of *Ipomoea eriocarpa* in Mali.

In 1993 Kew began a ten-year project in collaboration with the National Herbarium of Cameroon in Yaoundé and the conservation charity Earthwatch UK to survey plants in the remote highland forests of the Kupe-Bakossi area. Before the survey the region was not considered particularly significant, but during the course of the work the scientists and Earthwatch volunteers discovered 50 new species of plants and fungi. These ranged from a diminutive fungus to huge rainforest canopy trees. Three new species of coffee, one new ebony and one new busy lizzie (*Impatiens*) were among the species that may prove economically important in the future. Kew project leader Martin Cheek named the scarlet-flowered *Impatiens* found beside a forest stream after its discoverer, Earthwatch volunteer

Matthew Frith. 'He brought in the little plant with a flower on and we were able to work out that it was a species not yet known to science. When we went back at another time of year we found lots more in flower. It's called *Impatiens frithii*.'

In all, the scientists counted 2440 species from an area of 2390 square kilometres (950 square miles), making this the top centre for plant diversity so far documented in mainland tropical Africa. Part of Kew's work is now focused on making local people aware of the importance of conservation. Previously the forest was under threat from illegal logging and encroaching farmland, but now the government is in the process of taking action to protect much of Kupe-Bakossi. 'It's very, very important that we get this area protected,' says Martin. 'Some 232 of the species are listed on the World Conservation Union's Red List of Threatened Species, and 81 are strictly endemic, so they're known from there but nowhere else in the world.'

Education is an important part of Kew's work abroad; after all, important habitats will only be saved if people living nearby realize the value of preserving them. In Bolivia, Kew is supporting a community-based conservation project to create a botanical garden in the department of Santa Cruz. Local landowners donated a 20-hectare (50-acre) area of cactus scrub on a hill above the village of Pulquina, and the organizers aim to supplement existing cacti and bromeliads with other local species. By developing the garden as an eco-attraction, they hope to raise awareness

ABOVE: Field scientists brave all weathers in their quest to collect plants.

ABOVE: Scientists
undertake a plant
survey on the
Idenau lava flow,
Cameroon.

of the local flora and promote conservation to visitors. Several local bodies are backing the project. Kew plans to help these partners conduct vegetation surveys, create management plans and propagate plants. The long-term aim is to cultivate cacti and bromeliads for sale. This will help provide a sustainable income for the garden, while relieving collecting pressure on wild populations.

Collecting seed for the future

While conservation of threatened species is Kew's overall goal, it has also instigated an ambitious seed-banking project that will act as an insurance policy for the world's wild flora. Based at Wakehurst Place, beside the 400-year-old estate that Kew leases from the National Trust in the heart of the Sussex countryside, the Millennium Seed Bank Project aims to stockpile seeds from 10 per cent of the world's flora by 2010. 'We have 10,000 species at the moment, which is 40 per cent of the target, but the seeds are now coming in very fast,' explains Paul Smith, the head of the Millennium

Seed Bank. 'We received over 3000 species this past financial year, and will take 3500 this year, so we will meet the target. We have formal partnerships with 45 institutions in 18 countries across the world with whom we share seeds and the research benefits derived from them. Then, on top of that, we have donation agreements with a number of other organizations. They send seed to us and we simply store it as a back-up.'

Today's seed-collecting forays are a far cry from the imperialistic ventures instigated by the likes of Sir Joseph Banks and Sir William Hooker. Kew predominantly uses collectors from the country in question, training local botanists to identify plants and gather suitable material. It collects only seeds that are considered a priority by its partner organizations. As Paul says, 'Kew's motivations for collecting have changed enormously. In the past there was much more of an emphasis on collecting for our own research; now we concentrate on working with partners on projects that are driven by conservation and sustainability goals. In most cases, countries want us to help them collect seeds from habitats that are threatened. We tend to focus on species that fall under the three Es: Endangered, Endemic or Economically important. It's very different from the old colonial Kew's way of walking into someone's country and telling them how they should do things.'

Kew does, however, give guidelines for collectors to follow when gathering seeds. It's important that they sample as many different populations of a species as possible to ensure a wide genetic variation. Within each population they collect from, the aim is to get material from a minimum of 50 individual plants. Ideally, the Millennium Seed Bank likes to receive 20,000 seeds per collection. With plants such as orchids, which produce masses of tiny seeds, that figure is easy to achieve, but with some species it is simply not possible. 'You can imagine with an orchid it's easy to collect a million seeds in ten minutes, but with a coconut, there's no way you're going to collect 20,000 of those – and besides, we wouldn't have space to store them,' laughs Paul.

Seeds arrive daily at the Millennium Seed Bank's

BELOW: *Bixa orellana* seeds collected in Mali are of great economic value.

futuristic steel and glass building at Wakehurst Place. Before the drying process can begin, they must be cleaned of fruit and husks, which takes place in a dedicated laboratory. In the airy room a white-coated scientist gently rubs husks away from seeds the size of a fingernail with an abrasive block while the 1980s' hit 'Going back to my roots' blares from a radio in the corner. A card gives information about the seeds being cleaned: they are from the prairie cord grass (*Spartina pectinata*), which grows in wet meadows and around ponds across the USA. A note penned in capitals in the corner of the card warns that the seeds are infested. This often happens, but isn't necessarily a problem if only a few seeds harbour creatures. However, if lots are affected and there's little hope that they will yield plants, they are destroyed. 'I received a lovely collection of Umbelliferae that were infested, and the larvae had hatched in the post,' says Steve Alton, UK coordinator in the seed bank's Conservation Department. 'When I opened the parcel a huge cloud of flies flew out and landed on my blinds.'

The scientists check the quality of seeds that arrive by attempting to germinate some of them. This involves placing them on trays of agar at 20°C (68°F) and waiting to see if shoots appear. If they do, the rest of the collection is accepted into the seed bank. If not, the scientists try to germinate seeds at various temperatures and in different light regimes. A wall of 30 or so machines that look much like domestic larder fridges enable them to play God and try to create conditions that will spark germination. The machines can be set at varying levels of humidity and programmed to warm up or cool down at different times of the day. The aim is to fool the seeds into thinking that they are experiencing their native conditions, such as the hot days and cold nights of the desert, or the warm, moist conditions of the tropics. Seeds that germinate live short lives, as they end up in a designated clinical waste bin that is sent to a nearby hospital and destroyed. This 'plant abortion' procedure ensures there is no chance for plant diseases or alien species to affect the UK's wild flora.

Seeds from a collection that passes quality control go into a drying room inside cotton or paper bags that allow the moisture gradually to seep out. A complex system sucks air out of the room, cools it, dries it and then flows it back in to maintain conditions of 15 per cent humidity and 15°C (59°F). Inside the room hundreds of orange plastic trays and cardboard boxes are stacked with jars of every seed imaginable. They give the impression of an old-fashioned sweet shop; some seeds

OPPOSITE: A King protea, *Protea cynaroides*, originally from South Africa, in Kew's Temperate House.

are apple-sized, some have leopard-print spots and others resemble brown, furry gob-stoppers. 'The 15 or so processing staff are divided into teams, and each team is responsible for a small number of partner countries, so they follow the seeds all the way through the process – checking them, inputting the data gathered in the field to the database, cleaning, and finally storing them in the deep-freeze,' explains Steve.

Only when a small probe tells the laboratory staff that the moisture content has dropped to 3 or 4 per cent are the seeds deemed ready to go to the final drying room with its en-suite freezers. This lies at the bottom of a steel spiral staircase behind a heavy, vault-like door. Staff place the seeds in appropriate-sized glass jars labelled with the bar codes allocated to the specimens when they were collected. All material is divided between two archives: a base set that is not touched, and an active set that the seed bank's researchers can access. There are three freezers opening off the drying room, each of which is maintained at a chilly -20°C (-4°F). Should these become full, a large cavity excavated out of the rock beyond the drying room provides space for six more of the bolt-on freezers.

Although Kew would like to store seeds from as many species as possible, only 80 per cent of plant species have seeds that can be dried. The plants that yield them are called 'orthodox'. The remaining seeds, termed 'recalcitrant', cannot tolerate being dried. Storing samples of these species is a complex procedure that has yet to be perfected. 'One of the reasons we concentrate on seeds from dryland habitats is because nearly all the seeds found in dry areas are likely to be orthodox,' explains Paul. 'They have the capacity to dry down and sit dormant in the soil and then come up when the rains come – and that means that we can dry them and put them in the freezer.'

Climate change and conservation

To date, the motivation behind storing seeds has primarily been driven by the need to save habitats affected by such activities as farming, logging and urban development. But the coming years are likely to see a change in focus towards protecting species affected by climate change. As Paul explains, 'We feel we have a big role to play in climate-change studies. The current project kicked off before climate change was a major issue, so currently no country we're working with is specifically targeting species

SOWING THE SEEDS OF HISTORY

Two plants standing in the corner of an incubator at Wakehurst Place are proof that seeds can last for at least 200 years. The leafy specimens, an acacia and a liparia, were germinated by the Millennium Seed Bank from seeds discovered at the National Archives near Kew. Papers accompanying the seeds show that they were collected by a Dutch botanist who was captured by the British off Cape Town in 1803. The wallet contained around 30 different species, including the brown-beard sugarbush (*Protea speciosa*), the glossy-eyed parachute daisy (*Ursinia cakilefolio* – see below) and the king protea (*Protea cynaroides*), South Africa's national flower. 'He'd collected about 30 species, all of them horticulturally important, so we think he knew what he was doing,' says Paul Smith. 'He was probably taking them back to Holland for the flower industry.'

Researchers updating the National Archives catalogue came across the seeds in a red leather notebook while exploring the High Court of Admiralty prize papers. The seeds were wrapped in paper envelopes labelled with their Latin names. The notebook bore the name Jan Teerlink from Flushing, Holland, who is thought to have collected the seeds from the Cape of Good Hope. Several Dutch ships were seized in the early nineteenth century and brought back to the UK. The papers ended up at the High Court of Admiralty because British sailors, who were awarded prize money for capturing foreign ships and their sailors, used them as proof of capture. The ship carrying Teerlink and his seeds is believed to have been the *Henrietta*, and papers in the collection show it had been on a journey to gather goods from around the world.

most vulnerable to climate change. But we feel there's an opportunity to do that, particularly in places like South Africa, where predictions suggest they'll lose 30–40 per cent of their Cape flora. We're currently supporting a South African PhD student who is looking at what kind of life strategy predisposes a species to extinction. For example, if you're a tree with a long generation time and you use an explosive-pod mechanism, which means you're only able to move 30 metres every 1000 years, presumably that's disadvantageous compared to being a wind-dispersed plant that produces millions of seeds. She's looking at those issues and whether we should be targeting particular species with certain life-history strategies.'

Whenever Kew collects seeds it also thoroughly assesses the population from which it takes them, estimating the number of individuals and noting the environmental conditions. This means that by 2010, when it has gathered seeds from 10 per cent of the world's flora, it will also have baseline data for those 40,000 plant populations. As Paul points out, this is likely to prove invaluable as a marker against which scientists will be able to measure climate-induced changes to species. 'If some of the apocalyptic scenarios that we read about climate change come true, if the predicted plant extinctions are going to take place, we need to be playing a major

role in monitoring that and keeping an eye on what's happening to our plant diversity. The banking of seed in a changing climate is critical as a back-up. Although our first choice would be to keep everything safe *in situ*, at least if we have seeds stored, we have the option of going down the road of restoration and reintroduction. We have 200 horticulturalists here who do nothing better than cultivating plants outside their normal habitats and if the global climate's changing, we're not going to be able to preserve habitats exactly as they are. We and the plants will have to adapt. Botanic gardens have got to be at the forefront of that. We've got to get away from simply being visitor attractions and instead provide technical services to enable us to restore habitats that are vital to people's lives.'

A helping hand from Kew

In 1995 the Soufrière Hills volcano on the Caribbean island of Montserrat rumbled into life for the first time in 400 years. Ash and rocks began intermittently raining down on the lush tropical vegetation that covered its flanks, and on Plymouth, the

BELOW: Plymouth, Montserrat's once vibrant capital city, is now a ghost town.

capital city that lay to the south. For two years the volcano sent out hot, fast-moving blasts of gas, rock and ash called pyroclastic flows, which destroyed buildings, plants and wildlife. The activity peaked in June 1997, when a dome of viscous lava that had been building on the side of the volcano suddenly collapsed, destroying most of the villages on the southwest side of the island. Scientists estimate that 4–5 million cubic metres (5–6 million square yards) of rock and ash were deposited almost overnight. Today, after a decade of volcanic activity, the southern two-thirds of the island is uninhabitable, and Montserratians have had to rebuild their lives in the northern part of the island or further afield.

Before the eruptions, Chances Peak in the Soufrière Hills was covered by some of the finest cloud forest in the Caribbean. Tree ferns, palms and heliconia thrived, providing a rich habitat for bats, lizards, butterflies and birds. Lower down, the fertile soils yielded crops of papaya, coconut, mangos and bananas, while mangroves thrived along the southern coastal strip. That all changed when the volcano began erupting. Emissions of hydrogen sulphide and sulphur dioxide mixed with water to form acid rain, which turned leaves brown and slowly killed the plants. With over half the island's vegetation now dead, it's possible that some indigenous species have been lost for ever. And because most of the written records of Montserrat's endemic plants were also lost when pyroclastic flows swept through the original botanic garden in

BELOW: This endemic frog is named the mountain chicken because some consider it a delicacy.

Plymouth in 1997, no one really knows what has been lost. 'There's one woody shrub we're on the lookout for, called *Xylozma serratum*,' says Colin Clubbe, head of Kew's UK Overseas Territories Team. 'It was only known to grow at one place that is now under a pyroclastic flow, so we may have lost that species.'

With volcanic activity having destroyed most of the southern forests and mountains, the Centre Hills area of Montserrat has become the last remaining habitat for numerous threatened species. Some, such as the Montserrat oriole, the mountain chicken (despite its name, a type of frog), the galliwasp lizard and the Montserrat orchid (*Epidendrum montserratense*) do not exist anywhere else. In June 2005 Montserrat was awarded funding from the Darwin Initiative (a small grants programme, funded and

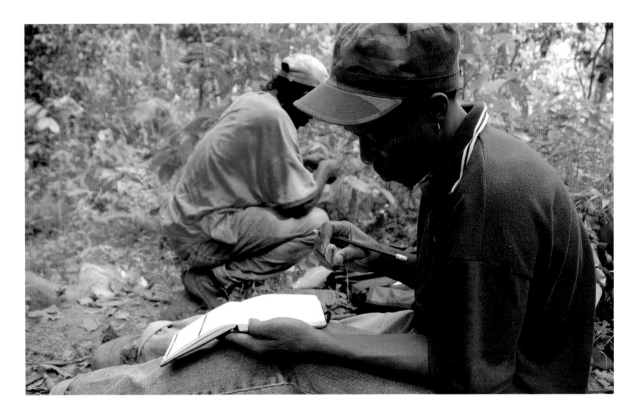

administered by the UK Department for Environment, Food & Rural Affairs – Defra – which aims to promote conservation and the sustainable use of resources around the world) to conserve the rich biodiversity of this mountain range. The Royal Botanic Gardens at Kew, the Royal Society for the Protection of Birds and the Durrell Wildlife Conservation Trust are working jointly with the Montserrat National Trust, Montserrat Tourist Board and the Ministry of Agriculture, Lands, Housing and Environment (MALHE) to work out how best to conserve the area.

'The first thing we're doing is a biodiversity assessment to find out what's there at a habitat level, so we're looking at the plants, birds, bats, insects, reptiles and amphibians,' explains Colin. 'We're also conducting a survey to find out what demands different sectors, such as agriculture and tourism, place on the Centre Hills. We'll use this information to create a management plan and maybe turn the area into Montserrat's first national park. On the plant side, Kew is going to produce an up-to-date vegetation map and create a "red list" showing what plants are threatened. And

ABOVE: Calvin 'Blacka' Fenton and Jervaine Greenaway gather information on Montserrat's flora at Cassava Ghaut.

RIGHT: Philemon
'Mappie' Murraine
is helping to create
a new botanic
garden for
Montserrat in the
grounds of a former
residential house.

because the botanical skills on the island are relatively few, we're also training people to collect and identify plants.'

Montserrat's woodlands range from dry forest at the coast to mesic (moist) semi-deciduous tropical forest at around 200 metres (660 feet), and upwards into mountainous cloud forest. Kew is helping to build up a detailed picture of the region's flora by taking samples of different plants gathered by Kew botanists and rangers from the Forestry Division of MALHE, identifying them and storing them in its Herbarium.

On an early morning foray into Cassava Ghaut on the western side of the Centre Hills, Darwin Initiative field officers Calvin 'Blacka' Fenton and Jervaine Greenaway gather samples from fruit trees to send back to Kew. As they crunch through dried leaves on a shady path dotted with boulders, Blacka points out the striking yellow flowers of heliconia (*Heliconia caribaea*), young coca saplings (*Erythroxylum coca*) and breadfruit trees (*Artocarpus altilis*) covered with elephant ear (*Philodendron giganteum*), an epiphyte so called because of its large leaves. 'We're looking to collect plants that are in flower or fruit, otherwise it's not possible to identify them,' explains Jervaine.

The first tree deemed suitable for gathering material is a banana of the *sikcri* variety that stands 4 metres (13 feet) high. The plant is taller and thinner than other species, with narrower leaves and thin-skinned, stubby fruits that are very sweet to taste. Jervaine records details about the plant in a notebook – from the height of its trunk to the rimy smell of the light green fruit – while Blacka uses a stick to separate a single banana from a bunch dangling above our heads. This is placed in a small plastic bag, which is inflated to prevent the fruit being squashed. Jervaine takes a portion of leaf and a dark pink segment of flower, sandwiches them between sheets of newspaper and stiff boards, and straps this temporary press into a specially designed canvas bag. The pair then repeat the procedure at a 30-metre (100-foot) mammee apple tree (*Mammea americana*), which Jervaine shins up to collect a few of the hard, orangey-brown, melon-sized fruits. He peels one and hands around slivers of the sweet, carrot-coloured flesh before writing in his notebook and carefully placing the samples in his field press.

Plans for Montserrat

'We're hoping we can set up a herbarium on Montserrat, so we're collecting everything in duplicate,' explains Colin. 'For the moment everything is being sent to Kew to be mounted, identified and verified, but we hope to find space at the National Trust's new headquarters on Montserrat so that the island can have its own national collection close at hand. The seed bank at Wakehurst is also taking material so that if a major eruption happens again, at least there will be some back-up.'

The National Trust moved into Olveston in the northwest of the island in the 1990s after the destructive pyroclastic flows forced all the inhabitants of Plymouth to leave for good. A cluster of white-painted buildings containing the trust's shop, museum, a replica of its former office in Plymouth and the Centre Hills Project's office stand around a red-tiled courtyard, with a veranda looking out across its 2.5-hectare (6-acre) grounds towards the azure sea. The trust's director, Lady Eudora Fergus, was awarded funding for the garden in 2005 from the Overseas Territories Environment Programme, a joint initiative by the UK's Department for International Development (DFID) and the Foreign Office. In consultation with Kew experts, the trust has drawn up plans for the plot and has started to transform the former residential garden into a national botanical resource. The aim is for it to become a centre for research, education and tourism. 'We need to preserve our natural indigenous plants, and we also want to widen our tourist base,' says Easton Farrell, who chairs the Botanic Garden Committee. 'The botanic garden will enable us to do both, as well as bringing in revenue for the National Trust.'

Before all that can happen, Philemon 'Mappie' Murraine has the task of turning the plot into a showcase of Montserratian and Caribbean plants. One cloudy April day he takes me on a guided tour, pointing out the various areas of the garden: a newly cut terrace that will become a lawn with tables, chairs and ornamental trees; the sections allocated to medicinal plants and Caribbean fruits, such as soursop (*Annona muricata*), sugar apple (*Annona reticulate*) and seaside grape (*Coccoloba uvifera*); a 'rainforest' area leading down to a pond; and a new nursery. Here and there he stops to point out plants currently in the garden. There's swibble sweet, a glossy-leaved citrus rootstock; pink-flowering frangipani (*Plumeria rubra*) and fragrant ylang ylang (*Cananga odorata*) trees; and shrubs such as the fiery orange and yellow pride of Barbados (*Caesalpinia pulcherrima*).

Down towards the bottom of the sloping garden is the tall fan of a well-established traveller palm (*Ravenala madagascariensis*) and a huge rambling ficus. 'The previous owner had put things wherever he felt like it,' explains Mappie. 'We'll have to take some things out, as well as adding more plants. The ficus is beautiful, but it will have to come out because this is only a small plot and it's taking up too much room.'

Mappie trained in propagation at the Forestry Division, but came to work at the National Trust seven years ago. Since the idea of the botanic garden was mooted in the early 1990s, he has worked tirelessly to prepare the ground and grow plants to both stock the garden and sell on. In his temporary nursery – essentially a wooden frame and chicken-wire roof covered with black mesh – an assortment of roses, crotons, purple allamanda (*Allamanda blanchetii*), bleeding hearts, bougainvillea and hibiscus stand in black polythene 'pots'; these ornamental plants will be sold to raise funds. When the new nursery is built at the bottom of the sloping garden it will incorporate an office, a display area for orchids, a composting zone and lots of space for propagating indigenous plants.

'Having identified what plants are endemic and threatened, we'll get those into cultivation as part of a recovery plan,' says Colin. 'We'll use the garden to raise awareness of plants that are unique to Montserrat and that need to be carefully conserved. In the long term we'd like to identify some plants that could form the basis of a cottage-scale sustainable industry, such as jewellery made from local plant materials, which could be sold in the shop.'

OPPOSITE: The red heliconia, *Heliconia caribaea*, is Montserrat's national flower.

Down the centuries innovative people have fashioned the bottle gourd (*Lagenaria siceraria*) into everything from musical instruments to penis shields. This hard-skinned fruit probably originated in Africa, but millennia-old artefacts made from gourds have shown up as far afield as Asia and the Americas. The large collection of gourds held in Kew's archives demonstrates the diversity of uses across countries in five continents (see below). It includes a water bottle from Beijing, China, dated 1878, a carved gourd pipe stem decorated with silver from India and a wine cask from Hungary.

One of the most unusual pieces is a gourd cage from Beijing, used for catching crickets. The creatures were encouraged to fight and bets were placed on who would be the victor. A note with the item, which dates from 1878, reads: 'The crickets carried in such cages are put into a conical-shaped bowl. In climbing the sides they fall and striking each other fight vigorously.' The gourd must have

been grown inside a mould because it has a pattern imprinted on its surface. The Chinese character repeated to create the pattern means 'happy', with particular reference to marriage.

The various species of gourd are all members of the cucumber family (*Cucurbitaceae*), and most are closely related to melons, pumpkins and squashes. Some have been used for medicinall purposes: their juice was used to prevent baldness and fight jaundice, and drinking an infusion of seeds was thought to cure chills and soothe headaches. In early Peruvian civilizations the bottle gourd was even used in surgery; parts of its shell were used to replace broken pieces of skull and the skin was stitched back over them.

Today there is concern that the diverse forms of the bottle gourd are disappearing. Modern wares, such as pottery and aluminium vessels, have replaced this natural one, prompting a decline in the gourd's importance and cultivation.

With conservation of the Centre Hills a key message for the new botanic garden to deliver, a focal point will be the rainforest zone, containing indigenous species that will lead visitors down to an ornamental pond. Currently the pool is empty but for a large rusting 'copper' – a pot once used on sugar plantations across the Caribbean to boil up molasses. Along the path sloping down to the pond are several red heliconias (*Heliconia caribaea*), Montserrat's national flower. Mappie hopes to supplement these with other moisture-loving tropical plants, such as tree ferns and bromeliads, and epiphytes, such as the impressive elephant ear. 'We want this to be a nice little jungle,' he explains. 'The water will come from a cistern at the top of the garden and will be gravity-fed down through the rainforest to the pond. I'm going to bring in plants from the wet, mesic and dry forests within the Centre Hills area. The garden is a dream that I want to make into a reality.'

Saving plant DNA for future generations

BELOW: Plant DNA is stored in the deep-freeze at Kew.

South Africa has one of the most diverse floras in the world. Some 20,000 vascular plant species occur within its boundaries, and many of these grow nowhere else. It is also the only nation to contain an entire plant kingdom, the Cape Floral Kingdom, which has the highest recorded species diversity for any similar-sized temperate or tropical region in the world. More plant species occur within the 22,000 hectares (55,000 acres) of Table Mountain National Park on the Cape Peninsula than in the whole of the British Isles. As with many African countries, however, rapid industrialization, population growth and urbanization pose a threat to the quality of the environment. For example, of the 9000 plants that grow in the Cape Floral Kingdom, scientists estimate that 1700 are threatened with extinction.

For the past three years scientists in Kew's Jodrell Laboratory have been working with the South African National Biodiversity Institute (SANBI) and the universities in Johannesburg and Cape Town to create a DNA bank in South Africa to house genetic material from the country's plants. As a safeguard, duplicates of the South African

RIGHT: Pincushion
proteas,
*Leucospermum
cordifolium*,
Cape Province,
South Africa.

samples will also be housed in the existing DNA bank at Kew. Inside a huge, humming freezer in Jodrell's DNA Laboratory, stacks of small trays hold vials containing individual DNA samples from the 25,000 species gathered from around the world and processed so far. A kind of hi-tech equivalent of dried specimens held by the Herbarium, these capsules of DNA are already in demand by scientists involved in taxonomy and conservation research projects. Kew's DNA bank is the largest store of genetic plant material from wild species in the world. At SANBI's DNA bank, scientists have received several requests from other African countries to help set up similar DNA stores.

'We've worked for three years on a Darwin Initiative programme to set up this DNA bank and make the DNA available for scientific research,' explains Vincent Savolainen, deputy head of Molecular Systematics at Kew. 'There are three areas of South Africa that have been identified as biodiversity hot spots: the Cape, the Succulent Karoo (a region of the Karoo desert that contains the richest biodiversity of succulents in the world) and the eastern part of the country near the Kruger National Park. We have gathered specimens from the Cape dry area, and now we're going to collect samples from Kruger, which is more of a savannah habitat.'

Preparing samples for the bank involves several processes. First, leaves, flowers or seeds are ground down using a pestle and mortar. A salt solution containing detergent is added to help break down the plant matter and release DNA. Next, the scientists add chloroform, which causes contaminant proteins to appear in the solution as solid matter. When the mixture is spun rapidly in a centrifuge, the DNA and salt solution become separated from the chloroform solution by a layer of solid proteins. The scientists can easily suck up the DNA from the unwanted solution in a pipette. Ethanol is used to precipitate out nucleic acids from the salt solution, and further purification is carried out if required. Eventually, the pure DNA is suspended in a solution and frozen at a temperature of -80°C (-112°F).

The bar-code project

DNA is a complex molecule made of sugar, nitrogenous bases and phosphorus bonds arranged in a double-helix pattern. The genome of every individual organism contains several thousand genes plus intra- or inter-gene 'spacers' all made up of DNA. A procedure called 'DNA bar-coding' has enabled biologists to successfully identify certain animal species using DNA taken from skin, fur or scales. The procedure uses a toaster-sized machine called a PCR thermocycler to produce billions of copies of stretches of DNA, then analyses them to sequence patterns that are specific to species populations, varieties or individuals. Now Kew scientists and their international colleagues are hoping they might be able to develop a similar DNA bar-coding procedure for plants, using material being gathered for the South African DNA bank in the Kruger National Park and elsewhere in the world.

'The DNA bar code is a short DNA sequence from a specific gene region, which can be used to identify species,' explains Robyn Cowan, a conservation genetics scientist at the Jodrell Laboratory. 'Researchers have found that one particular gene region is quite effective as a means of identifying animal species. But although plants have that same gene region, it doesn't evolve quickly enough, so we need to find another one or two regions that will perform the same function in land plants. The region you use needs to be evolving and mutating quickly enough so that changes show up from one species to another.'

Traditional techniques for identifying plant species rely on visual recognition of certain morphological structures. Currently, there is a worldwide shortage of taxonomists, so getting an accurate identification of a species can be time consuming. Simply gathering suitable plant specimens can be tricky, as they can only be identified when seeding or bearing fruit, so they must be gathered at these stages of their life cycle. With DNA, samples can be taken from any part of the plant at any time of the life cycle. And thanks to the PCR machine's ability to generate billions of copies of DNA sequences, only small samples of material are required.

Ultimately, the means to identify plants purely from DNA could lead to the development of a hand-held device capable of analysing and identifying species *in situ*. This would mean that Peter Gasson and his team in the Micromorphology Laboratory would be able to check the provenance of seized plants or wood as they arrive in the country; that Monique Simmonds and her staff could quickly verify the different plant species present in plant-based remedies or essential oils; and that forest rangers working in countries such as Montserrat could rapidly make a vegetation map without needing to undergo in-depth training or enlist experts. In short, if the bar-code project is a success, it could completely revolutionize plant identification across all fields of botanical science.

WILD WORK

AS THE SUN FADES ON AN EARLY summer's evening, Steve Robinson leads a wildlife-themed tour around Wakehurst Place's Loder Valley Nature Reserve. Kew leased Wakehurst Place and the adjoining reserve from the National Trust in 1965 to be the focus of its conservation efforts. Entry to the reserve is limited, so adult education natural history evenings are a popular way for people to explore the 60 hectares (150 acres) of ancient woods, wetlands and meadows. When Steve, who is warden of the reserve, reaches a spot beside Ardingly Reservoir, he disappears into the trees, emerging moments later with a wooden box and partially inflated clear polythene bag. Inside the bag is a honey-coloured dormouse with thick furry tail, beady black eyes and long, quivering whiskers. And inside the box is the rodent's nest, a cosy circle of thinly shredded honeysuckle bark. 'This is a hazel, or common, dormouse,' says Steve, who is licensed by English Nature to handle the protected

species. 'There are many species found across Europe, Africa and even Japan, but this one lives only in England. It was once a common Victorian pet, pre-dating hamsters and gerbils. But it's since become extinct in six English counties. Now the only strongholds are south of the Thames and Severn rivers.'

Dormice numbers have declined as their traditional habitat of coppiced hazel woodland has dwindled over the past 100 years. Before the Industrial Revolution, the UK's coppicing industry supplied timber for building, fencing and shipbuilding, as well as charcoal for cooking and heating. But when metals replaced wood as the favoured material in many industries, coppicing declined. Subsequent urban developments and new roads have since carved up remaining woodlands, and the corresponding reduction in biodiversity has made it impossible for some species, such as dormice, to thrive. 'Dormice are arboreal, meaning that they travel only above the ground using trees or hedgerows,' explains Steve. 'I layed this hedge you see before us about five or six years ago, and every winter I've found a dormouse nest in it. This shows that the dormice are using it as a thoroughfare. If you put a bypass through here, they could end up stranded, without sufficient diversity to survive.'

Woodland management

The woodlands of the reserve are the remnants of a great forest that stretched in Roman times from Kent to Hampshire. Its origins lay in the ancient wildwood that spread across the country after the retreat of the last ice age, some 10,000 years ago. Early humans soon learnt that they could harvest wood by coppicing, which involves cutting the trunks of trees to ground level and letting shoots grow up from the stumps or 'stools'. The practice keeps woodland open, letting understorey plants and wild flowers become established. In the Francis Rose Reserve, a section of the Loder Valley Nature Reserve designated a Site of Special Scientific Interest because of its unique sandstone rock habitats, a series of hollows beside the reservoir are evidence that people were coppicing trees and burning charcoal here hundreds of years ago. Today Steve has reverted to using this traditional form of woodland management to try to increase the biodiversity.

BELOW: Dead wood provides a rich habitat for fungi and insects.

'It's a 1000-year-old form of woodland management, and it creates a very diverse habitat,' he explains. 'In the 1940s and 50s the coppicing industry died away. The wood and charcoal were no longer needed, plus many of the men who worked the woods were killed in World War II. The woodlands then became neglected. What we're trying to do now is bring these woodlands back into this management system. Kew and Wakehurst use thousands of beanpoles and pea sticks, so we are coppicing the wood to produce those. It takes ten years to get the wood to the length and diameter that is useful, so we

ABOVE: This hedge was layed using coppiced poles from the woods at Wakehurst Place.

have ten blocks and we cut one every year on a rotational basis. When you first cut a block, you get bluebells and cuckoo flowers. That's good for butterflies and bees. As the shoots start growing up, they shade out ground flowers, so you get honeysuckle and brambles. Dormice use the nectar from honeysuckle flowers for food, and the bark for their nests. It's like having convenience stores dotted round the woodland.'

Steve also uses traditional methods to construct hedges. This involves 'pleaching' – cutting a wedge from the base of young trees and bending them over until they lie along the ground. Sufficient wood is left to keep the trees alive, and they then send up vertical shoots from dormant buds, which go to create the hedge. Posts set in the ground and woven with effers (horizontal poles) give the hedge structure in its early years. In the past, all field boundaries were made this way, which created a huge demand for coppiced poles. But as agriculture became mechanized, the hedges were removed to make fields bigger, and metal fences were used instead. 'Between 1945 and 1970, around 140,000 miles of hedges were removed – that's the same distance as going to Sydney and back four times,' says Steve. 'Now they're protected. They're very important for wildlife. As well as dormice using them to travel between woodlands, there's evidence that bats use them for echo location. As the young hedges thicken up, they're good for nesting birds, and you get mice, stoats and weasels using them too.'

Encouraging wildlife

Steve monitors the numbers of different creatures at Wakehurst Place to ensure that the management practices he is using are having the desired effect of increasing biodiversity. He records butterfly populations by walking along set transects and noting the species he sees. This information is sent to Butterfly Conservation, a British charity, for adding to their national database. 'It's useful to monitor butterfly numbers as they can be indicators of pollution,' he explains.

Since 1998, phenological data gathered in the Loder Valley has been submitted to the national programme coordinated by the Centre for Ecology and Hydrology. Phenology is the science of recording seasonal events in nature, such as the first cuckoo flower in spring or the arrival of the blackcap, a warbler that is increasingly wintering in the UK. This is useful for monitoring long-term changes in the climate. Steve also contributes data to English Nature's Species Action Plan for Dormice, and actively tries to increase their numbers at Wakehurst. The nesting box from which he lifted the dormouse to show visitors on the guided tour is one of 300 that are fixed to trees around the reserve.

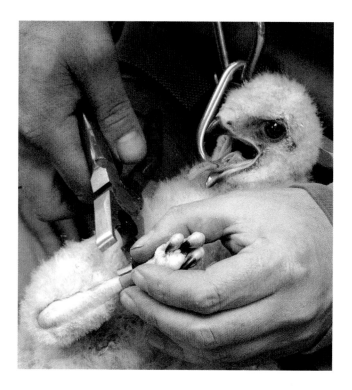

These nesting boxes have their entrance hole at the back, unlike bird boxes, but they nonetheless attract a number of feathered visitors. A quick trawl of a few reveals a cluster of brown and white spotted nuthatch eggs in a nest of birch bark, and a clutch of eight tiny great tits, hungry for food. 'We always get one or two boxes with hornets nesting in them, but the most unusual inhabitant I found was a toad,' says Steve. When he checks the boxes, he rings any birds he finds and sends the species data to the British Trust for Ornithology. Around 105 bird species live in or visit the Loder Valley Nature Reserve, including buzzard, reed bunting, woodcock and tawny

owl. 'If we didn't ring birds, we wouldn't know very much at all about them,' says Steve, gently lifting one of the tiny tits out of its nest. 'I ringed this young great tit this morning. Each ring has a number and the date and place it was ringed. And each species has its own size of ring; this one's a "B" ring. If this tit is found in Newbury in ten years' time, whoever finds it will know it is a decade old. I found a great tit today that was ringed beside the Bluebell Railway, near the border of East and West Sussex, seven years ago.'

Kingfishers are quite rare in southern England, but thrive at Wakehurst. To encourage them to breed in the reserve, the woodland and conservation team built an artificial kingfisher bank beside a quiet part of Ardingly Reservoir. By using one part cement to 100 parts sand, they created a wall that was soft enough for the kingfishers to burrow into it and build nests, but stable enough not to collapse. Just across the water from the bank, the team constructed a hide from pine logs, to which Steve leads this evening's group.

As we sit in the darkness, with a cool breeze blowing through the narrow opening that allows us to watch the birds, it's not long before a flash of turquoise and orange heralds the arrival of the first kingfisher. This is male, as it lacks the characteristic

BELOW: A kingfisher sits momentarily on a branch before delivering a fish to its waiting young.

orange strip that females display on the underside of their bills. With a sliver of silvery fish in his beak, he sits for a few seconds on a spike of dead wood above the water, then swoops into one of seven holes that perforate the bank. A few seconds later he's back, minus the fish. He sits briefly on the wood, then dips into the water before flying off to catch another meal. 'The kingfishers feed the fish head first to their young,' Steve explains. 'They're small fry of roach or bream. Sometimes I've seen them with fish almost as long as their own bodies.'

With the success of the kingfisher breeding bank, Steve created a raft to place on the reservoir in the hope of encouraging common terns (*Sterna hirundo*) to breed there. These silvery-grey and white birds have long tails that have earned them the nickname 'sea swallows'. They have a buoyant, graceful flight and frequently hover over water before plunging down for fish. They breed on shingle beaches, rocky islands and salt marshes along coasts, or on islands in gravel pits and rivers. Steve's shingle-covered raft on the reservoir was an instant hit; one pair took up residence almost immediately and produced three chicks. 'It's the first record of terns breeding at Wakehurst,' he says, proudly. The terns did not show their appreciation for their specially prepared breeding ground when he went to ring the new chicks, however. 'Terns don't like humans approaching their breeding sites, so usually they swoop down and just miss your head,' he says. 'But last year, when I was rowing out to them, one of them struck me and I ended up bleeding so much that I couldn't see where I was rowing. Next time I'm going to take my motorcycle goggles and chainsaw helmet just in case.'

At the edge of the reservoir within the Francis Rose Reserve, Wakehurst Place staff are busily constructing a timber-framed building. Two of the team went to the Weald and Downland Open Air Museum at Singleton to learn how to build wooden-framed buildings using traditional oak pegs and dowels. So far, the wall and roof timbers are in place, but the 1400 hand-shaped shingles (wooden roof tiles) have yet to be laid. Much of the wood came from oak 'standards' – mature trees growing within the coppice blocks. In olden times it was standard practice to grow such trees within coppiced woodlands. The underwood suppressed the lower side-branches of the standard trees, thus encouraging the growth of tall, unbranched trunks suitable for use in major construction projects, such as shipbuilding. During the reign of Henry VIII (1509–47), the law dictated that at least 12 standards per acre (30 per hectare) be grown.

'Access to this part of the woodlands is restricted because it's a Site of Special Scientific Interest, but it's very interesting and beautiful, so we decided to let people enter in a controlled way,' explains conservation and woodlands manager Iain Parkinson. 'The building will be like an information centre. The trees in front will be thinned out so that people will be able to get really good views of the birds. There are common buzzards, herons, lots of mallard, coots, moorhens and mandarin ducks.'

Visitors good and bad

Behind the skeletal building is an area of deciduous woodland, where Steve points out an old, dead beech tree that is fast becoming a haven for wildlife. Insects and beetles have infiltrated the nooks and crannies in the dead wood, and where the bark is peeling off tree creepers will probably soon move in. Although there are new young beeches growing around the dead one, they are unlikely to reach maturity, he explains, because of a less welcome wild visitor to Wakehurst – the grey squirrel. 'Grey squirrels strip the bark off beech trees, and if they remove it right the way round the upper part of the tree or branch – called "ring-barking" – it will die. These mature beech trees are 200 years old. Grey squirrels were only introduced into the UK 150 years ago, so the big trees pre-dated them and weren't touched. But we'll never see those big old beech trees in this woodland again – all because of grey squirrels.'

Another mammal that has caused a few problems at Wakehurst in recent years is the badger. Although the increase in badgers on the estate has been a welcome result of the woodland management regime, one of the animals decided to excavate a sett close to the mansion. Improvements made to the appearance of the lawns had prompted an increase in the number of worms, and as these are a favourite food of the badger, the creature wasted no time in digging up the grass on the croquet lawn to sniff them out. Fortunately, when the lawns dried out in spring the worms retreated too deeply for the badger to smell, so the gardeners were able to restore the lawn to its former glory. So far the wayward badger has not returned.

Wakehurst has a further 20 setts, containing 60 or more badgers, but these are located in the heart of the woodland. A new hide was recently built in front of where the setts are concentrated to increase the number of people who could see them. 'We've been running badger-watching evenings for ten years now,' says Steve, as he

OPPOSITE: Badgers, like these ones at Wakehurst Place, are nocturnal, leaving their setts at dusk to seek supplies of juicy earthworms.

leads tonight's tour to its finale at the hide. 'In the seven years I've been doing it, I've only *not* seen a badger once.'

This evening's group is not disappointed. As dusk falls, a small black-and-white striped head pops up from the sandy opening of one huge sett. It disappears for a few moments before appearing again, followed by the badger's lumbering, brindled body. The creature stretches sleepily, then runs athletically up the wooded bank behind the sett and out of view. Another follows suit soon afterwards. 'They're a bit like humans when they wake up,' says Steve. 'The first thing they do is have a scratch, then run to the latrine, but hopefully they'll come back.'

Soon several other badgers leave the sett and go about finding food. Steve has sprinkled a few peanuts in front of the hide and around the entrance to the sett, and soon seven individuals are sniffing energetically around the ground and hoovering up the calorific morsels one by one. Two of the animals are only a few months old, and roll around the ground in play fights as they battle to get to the nuts. Another pair – possibly their parents – begin copulating beside the sett entrance. The scene, viewed from behind a wide glass window in the hide, is like watching a David Attenborough documentary on wide-screen TV – except it's for real.

Badgers are creatures of habit, and follow regular paths through fields, woods and meadows as they travel between their setts and foraging grounds. They continue using these routes even when roads are driven through them, and, as a result, the car has become their greatest threat. In Britain around 50,000 badgers die in traffic accidents every year. The animals are able to thrive at Wakehurst because the woods provide a safe haven that is relatively distant from main roads. About 65 kilometres (40 miles) to the northwest, Kew's walled gardens are also proving a hit with badgers – so much so that their numbers have risen rapidly in recent years. They generally emerge at dusk after the last visitors have left, but leave plenty of evidence of their presence. Well-trodden pathways show their nightly forages, as do scratch marks on trees and hairs caught on fencing. Sometimes they leave nesting material from their setts out to air.

'Kew is crammed to bursting with badgers,' says Sandra Bell, wildlife and environment recording coordinator. 'There are over 20 setts, which equates to some 70 or 80 individuals. They came to Kew via Richmond Park and along the towpath, and because there aren't many places they can go towards London, they're at something of a bottleneck here. We can't do very much about it because the level of protection given to them by the government is quite high. So if they choose to burrow under a prized tree, all we can do is propagate it and let them get on with it. But it's enjoyable to have them around.'

Keeping records

Sandra is responsible for ensuring the wild flora and fauna at Kew is monitored, surveyed and recorded. It's a big task because of the sheer size of the gardens, and the array of exotic plants means a wide range of animals live there. There are 40 resident bird species, plus 30 seasonal visitors, 23 species of butterflies, and nine species of dragonfly, along with 400 native and naturalized wild flowers. Many of the species are monitored according to national data-gathering protocols. 'For some species, such as dragonflies and damselflies, we use the system developed by the British Dragonfly Society and feed information into their national recording scheme,' explains Sandra. 'For others it's a case of organizing a one-off survey. For example, we've just carried out an individual survey of lichens. That data can be compared

BELOW: The presence or absence of butterflies can indicate the health of a habitat.

with surveys that were done 60 and 100 years ago. Kew is really very special; there are many, many things here that don't occur anywhere nearby because of the way London has developed. For example, we have some very unusual soldier flies that you'd have to go a very long way to find elsewhere. And we still have the white-letter hairstreak butterfly here, which has declined dramatically around the rest of the country because of Dutch elm disease. In almost every group of plants or animals you look at you'll find things here that are very special; that's one of the exciting things about working at Kew.'

Butterflies are very good indicators of the health of invertebrates' habitats, and by studying their fluctuations year on year against national trends, Kew staff can work out whether the gardens' management techniques are appropriate, and if not, take remedial action. Like Steve Robinson at Wakehurst Place, Sandra or one of her team walks fixed transects every week, recording the numbers of different species encountered. 'A lot of our butterflies have larval stages that feed on grass, particularly longer grass,' she says. 'There's obviously plenty of grass out there, but what may cause problems is when you cut it. If you cut at the wrong time and take the mowings away, you may well decimate certain populations of butterflies. So you have to learn which species are where and adapt the mowing regimes so that they have a good chance of completing their life cycles and building up their numbers from year to year. We maintain areas of sward containing long grass and other wild flowers in a state that many butterfly species can use in the larval stage. It's quite a complex science. For example, you can have acres of the food plant in very exposed positions and the butterflies won't use any of it because they love sunny, sheltered microclimates.'

Keeping things natural

On the southern side of Kew, Simon Cole, manager of the Natural Areas, is dealing with one part of the gardens in a way that specifically encourages wildlife. The Natural Areas cover 16 hectares (40 acres) and comprise a designated conservation area and the former grounds of Queen Charlotte's Cottage. When Queen Victoria gave the building and its surroundings to Kew in 1898, it was her wish that the grounds be left in a wild, natural state, which to a large extent they have. Nevertheless, some changes have taken place in the intervening years. Around the turn of the twentieth century

TIME FOR A BAR-B-KEW

In a clearing in the woods at Wakehurst Place's Loder Valley Nature Reserve are two rusting circular containers about 3 metres (10 feet) across. These are the burners in which warden Steve Robinson creates charcoal from some of the more mature wood he generates from managing the woodland (see below). 'We've been opening up the rides through Wakehurst, cutting an artery through the reserve to let the light in and bring back wild flowers,' he explains. 'The wood you see in the kiln has come from the trees we've taken from the edge of the route.'

The wood is placed in the kiln so that it all lies in one direction. Around 4 tonnes of wood will generate around 0.5 tonnes of charcoal; the other 3.5 tonnes are lost as water and volatiles evaporate. The kiln is enclosed with a lid, which restricts the oxygen and raises the burning temperature to around 300°C (572°F). It is left for 24–30 hours, depending on how dry or wet the wood is. At the end, the kiln is full of charcoal – essentially the carbon skeleton of the wood that went into it.

'We send the ashes up to Kew for improving the soil quality,' says Steve. 'The rest we bag up and sell as barbecue charcoal under the brand name Bar-B-Kew. In the UK we have a huge resource that could be converted to charcoal, but 90 per cent of the charcoal people buy is imported from Africa and South America, where it is harvested from unsustainable woodland. We try to educate people to use English lump-wood charcoal to help sustain our woodlands.'

several broad, straight rides were driven through the area surrounding the building, to the east of the path leading to the King's Steps Gate. And in 1914 some 150 oak, poplar, birch and Douglas fir trees were planted in the cottage grounds. Lilies, snowdrops, primroses and narcissi were added in 1958, while 35 English oak saplings were planted in 1984 to launch the 'Beautiful Britain' campaign. Subsequently, the grounds had been barely managed until Simon took over his role as manager of the Natural Areas three years ago. 'I've been restoring lots of the historic rides that have closed in, reclaiming grassland from scrub, increasing the dead-wood quantities around the conservation area as a whole, and planting new hedges,' he says. 'In terms of conservation, it's the most improved area of the gardens.'

On a walk through the area Simon points out some of his improvements. To one side of a grassy ride dense, dark stands of rhododendrons have shaded out all the other plants, leaving the beds looking bleak and forbidding. On the opposite side, where he has removed rhododendrons and planted young trees, new 'pioneer' plants are making the most of the exposed soil. Further along, among the oak trees, is one of the best carpets of bluebells in London. Several limp piles of the invasive weed *Smyrnium perfoliatum* sit beside the path, pulled out by volunteers over the weekend in an effort to encourage the growth of the bluebells. They are not all native English ones, however. A close inspection reveals that some are the introduced Spanish species. Simon explains that the English ones have a curved stem with delicate blue flowers on only one side. The Spanish ones have a straight stem with flowers all the way round. 'The majority are English bluebells but we are also seeing hybrids of the two here,' he says. 'We have to go with the flow a little bit; this is a future nature we're looking at. But it would be sad if we lost all our native bluebells.'

One of the ways in which Simon is encouraging native species is by increasing the amount of dead and decaying wood around the Natural Areas. When trees die, rather than raze them to the ground he removes the branches but leaves the trunks standing. And instead of slicing off the top to leave a smooth platform, Simon practises 'coronet pruning'. This leaves a jagged edge that provides nooks and crannies for insects to hide in. As the bark decays and comes away from the trunk, it creates suitable cavities for tree creepers and other small birds to nest in. 'Generally, I let nature take its course as much as possible,' he says. 'Over there you can see the jagged tops of beech branches. The tree just crashed down one day, but it's still very much alive. If I cut it down, I'd be breaking it off before the end of its life cycle. A tree is

only gone when you can't see it any more. Britain is lucky to have a high percentage of ancient trees. Thankfully, we're waking up to that now, and environmental movements have developed to raise awareness of their value. They harbour so much really important wildlife.'

In a clearing along the southern edge of the Natural Areas is a collection of tree trunks arranged vertically to form a kind of organic Giant's Causeway. Simon rescued them from across Kew and built the 'loggery' to encourage saproxylic insects – those that feed on decaying wood. The creature he's most keen to attract is the stag beetle; two giant ones carved from wood sit atop the logs to draw the attention of passing visitors. This globally endangered beetle has declined rapidly across the UK as a result of the trend for tidying up fallen branches in parks and gardens; its larvae live in dead wood for up to seven years while they are maturing.

In urban areas traffic, feet, cats and other predators have also had a detrimental impact. Despite having fearsome-looking antlers that are actually jaws, stag beetles are harmless and play an important role in returning minerals from dead plants to the soil. Although rare across northern parts of the UK, they are holding out in southern England, especially the Thames Valley, north Essex, south Hampshire and West Sussex. In London they are concentrated in Bromley, Croydon and Lewisham. Simon belongs to the Steering Group for Stag Beetle Conservation in London, and the loggery is part of the Species Action Plan for Stag Beetles in the capital. 'If everyone put one of these loggeries in their garden, it would go some way to increasing the population across London,' he says.

Minding its own backyard

Simon has also given a helping hand to water-loving insects and amphibians by creating a pond close to the river Thames at the southwest tip of the gardens. Two local schools – Unicorn and Queen's Church of England – assisted him. At the start of the project he ran assemblies for the pupils and encouraged them to come up with drawings of what they'd like to see. The circular pond, with its wooden platform, three small beaches and giant wooden carvings of a frog, dragonfly and crested newt, is the result. Simon planted a ring of native woodland plants around the water's edge,

LEFT: A recently emerged common darter dragonfly.

but has deliberately not introduced any livestock because he wants the pond to be populated naturally. A quick dip with a net into the water reveals that racing water-boatman, mayfly and damselfly have already set up home among the greater reedmace (*Typha latifolia*) and branched bur-reed (*Sparganium erectum*).

'In about July the dragonflies will be crawling up those grass stems and hatching out into adults,' he says. He is hoping that frogs and newts will also make use of the pond, and has sunk small boxes, complete with entrance tunnels and wooden lids, into the ground in the hope of encouraging them. So far, perhaps because of the surfeit of hungry badgers, they have kept away. 'We found a metre-long grass snake in one of the boxes, though,' he says.

Close to the pond is a wide pit that was dug in the late 1960s, when gravel was needed for the foundations of Kew's original Alpine House. At first the pit was regularly flooded by overflow from the Thames, but that hasn't happened for several years. Its soils are alluvial gravels and sand, which are low in nutrients. These unusual conditions have attracted brambles, nettles, pink comfrey and other plants to form a self-contained habitat within the hollow. There are rare bog plants in the pit's soggy bottom, and the sandy sides are home to bee colonies. Badgers have also built a sett in the side of the pit. Although visitors to the conservation area are asked to stay on the tarmac paths to help protect vulnerable species from being trampled, they can observe the wild inhabitants of the pond and gravel pit from a specially constructed wooden viewing platform.

Throughout the Natural Areas of Kew Gardens, and in the Loder Valley Nature Reserve at Wakehurst Place, the application of traditional woodland management practices is showing that it is possible to increase biodiversity by nurturing conditions in which Britain's native species can thrive. Rare species, such as the carnivorous slug (*Testacella baliotidea*) and the two-lipped snail (*Balea biplicata*) have been recorded at Kew, kingfishers and dormice are thriving in the Loder Valley, and the increase in dead wood at both locations is proving a hit with stag beetles and fungi alike. Eighty species of fungi have been noted in the loggery in recent years, ranging from a type of stereum, which looks like elegant Arabic writing, to edible oyster mushrooms.

'Part of Kew's remit is to encourage botanical gardens around the world to conserve their indigenous species,' says Steve Robinson. 'It was the first such garden to have its own nature reserve. By using traditional management practices to encourage native species on the Wakehurst estate and in the Natural Areas, it is showing that it's doing its bit for conservation in its own backyard.'

One of the most valuable books in Kew's collection is the *Metamorphosis Insectorum Surinamensium* by Maria Sibylla Merian (1647–1717). Maria's upbringing was influenced by her artist stepfather Jacob Marell, who made sure she was taught to draw and paint. Fascinated by metamorphosis, she drew caterpillars alongside their species-specific food plant, their own cocoon or pupa and the emerging butterfly. In 1685 Maria converted to Labadism, a mystical offshoot of Catholicism, and took her two daughters to live in a Labadist colony in Holland, at the castle owned by the governor of the Dutch colony of Surinam in South America. Fascinated by his cabinet of exotic butterflies and insects, 52-year-old Maria decided to travel to Surinam to study the country's insects and flora.

After two years in the wilderness, she returned to Europe and produced *Metamorphosis Insectorum Surinamensium*, documenting the full life cycles of Surinam's insects and the native plants on which they lived. The first edition was published in 1705 with 60 plates; a further 12 were added to later editions. The prints provided Europeans with the first extensive visual record of the exotic colours and forms of the plant and insect life of South America. The work's scientific accuracy, Maria's blending of entomological and botanical elements, and the illustrations' fine decorative appearance made the book an instant success. Today Maria's prints remain among the most desirable of all natural history images. The volume in the library at Kew Gardens is a first edition coloured by Maria herself (see right).

GRAND DESIGNS

FROM FOLLIES AND FLAGPOLES TO GRAND glasshouses and palaces, architecture has always been integral to Kew. While many buildings have long gone, those that remain reflect the changing fashions and functions of the gardens over the years. In the early eighteenth century, when Kew still comprised the two adjoining estates of Kew and Richmond, follies and decorative buildings were in favour. William Kent designed those at Richmond, while William Chambers was architect at Kew. Indeed, Kew was famed for follies being constructed overnight, but most were flimsy and did not last. Only the Ruined Arch and the temples of Bellona, Arethusa and Aeolus remain of these frivolities. Later, as Britain began to colonize the world, it became fashionable to show off designs and features from far-flung places. William Chambers' ten-storey Pagoda, once the most accurate imitation of a Chinese building in Europe, dates from this time.

Acquiring gravitas

As Kew became involved with more serious scientific and economic endeavours, it began sending plant collectors across the globe to gather seeds and saplings for it to propagate. This prompted the need for facilities in which to re-create the environmental conditions of the plants' natural habitats. The Orangery, which is now a restaurant, was one of the early, experimental glasshouses. But it is the hothouses commissioned by Sir William Hooker for which Kew has become renowned. Designed by Decimus Burton, in partnership with ironfounder Richard Turner, the Palm House and Temperate House are masterpieces of Victorian engineering. Now both well over 100 years old, they are still brimming with palms, ferns, cycads and citrus trees. In fact, the Palm House contains one of the oldest pot plants in the world – a specimen of the cycad *Encephalartos altensteinii* brought to Kew from South Africa by Francis Masson in 1775.

Some of the main elements of the structured landscaping seen at Kew today were the work of William Andrews Nesfield. A talented watercolourist and landscape gardener, Nesfield worked on over 260 estates belonging to the wealthiest and most

influential people of the day. When Kew asked him to redesign the Arboretum in 1844, he introduced the Broad Walk with alternating cedars and flowerbeds, remodelled the landscape around the emerging Palm House and created the Syon and Pagoda vistas. Over the years more buildings have sprung up in his stately landscape. They include the Evolution House (previously called Australia House), the Princess of Wales Conservatory, the newly extended Jodrell Laboratory, the Sir Joseph Banks Building for Economic Botany and the Victoria Gate visitor centre.

In 2006 Kew celebrated its heritage with a series of events linked to its landscape and architecture. These included restoring and opening the Pagoda and Kew Palace to the public, marking the footprint of the White House in which Frederick, Prince of Wales lived with Kew's founder, Princess Augusta, rebuilding follies, and re-creating a menagerie stocked with wallabies. In a continuation of the tradition for showcasing creative contemporary architecture at Kew, two new buildings were also unveiled. The Davies Alpine House now exhibits delicate alpine plants, such as saxifrages, primulas and tulips, while the elegant Sackler Crossing has enabled visitors to cross the lake at the west end of the gardens for the first time.

ABOVE: Richard Turner, the ironfounder who helped design the Palm House and Temperate House.

The Palm House

Suddenly the sunrise ran a long band of glowing saffron over the shadow to port, and the vague summit became remarkable with a parapet of black filigree, crowns and fronds of palms and strange trees showing in rigid patterns of ebony. A faint air then moved from off shore as though under the impulse of the pouring light. It was heated and humid, and bore a curious odour, at once foreign and familiar, the smell of damp earth, but not of the earth I knew, and of vegetation, but of vegetation exotic and wild. For a time it puzzled me that I knew the smell; and then I remembered where we had met before. It was in the palm house at Kew Gardens. At Kew that odour once made a deeper impression on me than the extraordinary vegetation itself, for as a boy I thought that I inhaled the very spirit of the tropics of which it was born.

Henry Major Tomlinson, *The Sea and the Jungle* (1912)

The elegant curved profile and exotic foliage of the Palm House have been enticing visitors to Kew for more than 150 years. When it opened in 1848 the glasshouse represented a milestone in building design, for it was the first time engineers had used wrought iron to span such widths without supporting columns. This technique, copied from the shipbuilding industry, created unobstructed space that could easily accommodate the crowns of large palms. Initially, palms, cycads and climbers were grown in teak tubs or clay pots, but in 1860 two central beds were dug and the tallest plants placed in them. During subsequent restorations in the 1950s and 1980s, most of the remaining plants were dug into beds, forming a miniature rainforest. Today, as in Victorian times, the steamy warmth and earthy scent, towering

BELOW: Workmen put the roof of the Palm House in place.

tree palms and creeping climbers transport visitors to the tropics as soon as they swing open the heavy iron doors.

Plans for a palm house were initially mooted in 1834, but it was not until after Sir William Hooker became Kew's first official director in 1841 that the idea became a reality. The architect Decimus Burton proffered plans for a cast-iron glasshouse that looked similar to his Great Conservatory at Chatsworth. However, ironfounder Richard Turner suggested using wrought iron, which would do away with the need for central supporting struts. The final design was an amalgamation of both men's visions.

To generate the warmth and humidity desired by tropical plants, boilers were installed beneath the building. A tunnel running from the Palm House basement to an Italian campanile-style chimney beside the Victoria Gate served the dual purpose of carrying away sooty fumes and enabling coal to be brought to the boilers by a hidden railway. The specification for the Palm House was for 'a temperature of 80 degrees during the coldest winter', but in its early days the heating system frequently malfunctioned and many a tender tropical plant withered in the chill.

Since the installation of a new heating system in the 1980s, water is warmed by boilers located in the Shaft Yard by Victoria Gate, then pumped along thick, insulated pipes down the tunnel to the Palm House. Sensors called 'psychrometers' located high up in the glasshouse constantly monitor the humidity and relay data to a computer located in a subterranean office close to the entrance of the tunnel. The regular watering of the beds tends to keep the level of moisture in the air relatively high, but if it drops below 70 per cent sprinklers automatically send out sprays of fine droplets to redress the balance. Similarly, if the temperature drops below 19°C (66°F), the computer relays a message for more heat to be pumped in. 'Even if the heating fails in the middle of the night, the computer will register this and send an alarm to security so they can call emergency engineers to come and fix it,' explains Palm House horticulturist Wesley Shaw.

Plants from tropical and subtropical parts of the world thrive in this warm, moist environment. The central beds beneath the dome are reserved for the world's tallest tree palms, which cannot be reduced in height without killing the point from which the plant grows – its 'heart'. The rest of the beds are divided geographically, with African plants in the south wing, those from the Americas in the main central section (except for the very tallest, which can be from anywhere), and specimens from Asia, Australasia and the Pacific in the north wing. Many are important sources of timber, food and medicines.

OPPOSITE: Water-lilies, *Victoria amazonica*, thrive in a specially designed glasshouse close to the Palm House.

In the past Kew helped Britain to achieve trading supremacy by distributing species such as coffee, rubber and tea around the globe for large-scale production on plantations. Today it is motivated by the need to preserve natural habitats. With 50 per cent of the cycad species and 25 per cent of palms exhibited in the Palm House threatened with extinction, the glasshouse is now a showcase for what could be lost if rainforests are not conserved.

Sometimes, however, even Kew has to chop down its own precious trees. Three or four times a year Wesley recognizes that a palm is growing too close to the roof of the glasshouse and has to make arrangements to remove it. One recent sacrifice was a towering talipot palm that was a present to the Queen from Sri Lanka in the 1960s. 'It's a great shame that we had to take it out because it's really only a juvenile; in the wild it would grow another 20 metres,' he explains. 'It's the national symbol of Sri Lanka and it's a fantastic palm because it has the largest flowering structure of any plant in the world. It grows a 7-metre tall spike with millions of flowers – and then it dies. But sadly, this one won't ever get the chance to bloom, as it would have to be here for another 70 or 80 years before that would happen. We'll just have to obtain some seed and hope we can propagate another one.'

The Arc and the Minka House

Such is the popularity of the Palm House at Kew that many visitors simply head straight there, wander around the lake and go home without ever seeing the gardens' other hidden highlights. Those who do venture further afield often walk the triangle formed by the Pagoda, Syon and Cedar vistas, but neglect the large central area and western edge of the gardens. The result is that while the Broad Walk, Orangery, Palm House and Victoria Gate visitor centre are often busy, the Rhododendron Dell, Woodland Glade and Azalea Garden are quiet, with barely a soul in sight. And so few visitors venture into the Japanese Minka House, deep in the Bamboo Garden, that a family of bats have made it their home.

Kew hopes to solve this problem by carving a new path through the heart of the gardens. Called the 'Arc', the path will take visitors from the Marianne North Gallery, through the Temperate and Evolution Houses to Capability Brown's Woodland Glade, then over the lake via the Sackler Crossing, past the Minka House and Bamboo

IN KEW'S ARCHIVES: **Palm House pictures**

Within Kew's valuable collection of photographs are two black-and-white images showing the Palm House during its construction. In one of the pictures, two men in top hats and tailcoats sit together inside the skeletal cavern of the structure (see below). One, a tall, thin gentleman, is perched on the edge of a large box with his arms crossed. The other, a more portly chap, is seated on a wheelbarrow. The images were uncovered several years ago by Kew's former librarian Ray Desmond, author of *The History of the Royal Botanic Gardens, Kew*, and an expert on the gardens' archives.

'When I appeared in the first series of *A Year at Kew* I showed the picture to the gardens' then director Sir Peter Crane, saying, "Here's your predecessor, Sir William Hooker",' explains James Kay, assistant illustrations curator in the Herbarium Library. 'Later Ray came up to me and said, "I don't think you're right. I think it's Decimus Burton and Richard Turner, the architects." It seemed that I'd been on TV for ten seconds and managed to say a load of rubbish. I felt terrible because Ray knows everything, and without him we wouldn't even have these important images in our collection.'

Ray suggested getting the images photographed and blown up, and when James saw the faces enlarged he thought that the gentleman on the right was definitely Sir William Hooker. But Ray still believed the pictures showed Burton and Turner. But then Ray had a change of mind and said he thought the men could be Sir William Hooker and his son Sir Joseph Hooker, who were both directors at Kew. 'So the current theory is that William is the guy on the right and Joseph is the younger chap on the left,' says James. 'But it's a rolling theory. Unless someone finds the document that accompanied the daguerreotypes we'll never know for sure.'

Garden and on to the Brentford Gate. The Sackler Crossing is Kew's first bridge, and was specially commissioned to enable the Arc to span the lake. The striking, black granite walkway is bounded by a series of flat, bronze posts. When you approach the bridge these give the appearance of forming a solid barrier on either side of the walkway. However, seen sideways-on from the western end of the lake, they are almost invisible, and the view to the eastern end is unobscured.

Tony Hall, who looks after Kew's woody plant collections, and Ray Townsend, the arboretum manager, have spent several months clearing away the dense vegetation in the Bamboo Garden, so when visitors now step off the western end of the Sackler Crossing they glimpse the roof of the Minka House close by. This unsung architectural gem came to Kew in 2001. A traditional Japanese farmhouse of the kind most ordinary people lived in until the middle of the twentieth century, it was donated by the Japan Minka Reuse and Recycle Association. The house was originally built around 1900 in a suburb of Okazaki City, near the southern coast of central Japan. Then, in 1940, the Yonezu family bought it and moved it to another part of the city. After their main house was destroyed by a bomb, they moved into the Minka House in 1945.

The last member of the family to live in the house was Mrs Chiyoku Yonezu. After she died in 1993, it was shipped to Kew and rebuilt by Japanese and local craftsmen, using traditional methods. The pine logs that make up the frame are lashed together with rope, the walls are made of wattle and daub, and the outside is limewashed a creamy yellow. The house, standing on a base of large stones, is held down by its own weight. Minkas were not historically cemented to their foundations because of the risk of earthquakes in Japan. Should a quake take place – although this is somewhat unlikely in its new setting – the house would simply move on its base rather than disintegrate.

As part of the work to relandscape the area immediately around the Minka House, Tony hopes to plant a specimen of *Morus alba*, which Japanese farmers traditionally used to raise silkworms. He has already dug in a series of young plants of *Nandina domestica* or 'sacred bamboo' that will grow to around 1 metre (3 feet) high and display fiery red hues in autumn. Despite its name, the plant is not a bamboo but an evergreen shrub, with berries that the Japanese traditionally used to treat influenza, coughs and upset stomachs. Beyond the house, Tony will be showcasing each of the Kurume azaleas that plant collector Ernest Wilson introduced to the USA from Japan in 1919. Known as 'Wilson's 50', these beautiful, showy plants will provide a colourful link to the adjacent Azalea Garden, which is situated to the north-east of the Bamboo Garden.

The Temperate House

Decimus Burton's Temperate House never achieved the iconic status of the Palm House, despite being the largest surviving Victorian glasshouse in the world. Covering some 4880 square metres (5850 square yards) and stretching to 19 metres (63 feet) high, it could accommodate the entire Palm House twice over, but some say it lacks its tropical counterpart's rounded elegance. Commissioned in 1859 to house Kew's burgeoning collection of semi-hardy and temperate plants, the Temperate House was not completed for 40 years because the costs soared during construction. When it was officially opened, unfinished, in 1863, its first inhabitants were some palms from the overcrowded Palm House, New Zealand specimens moved from the crumbling, century-old Great Stove and tubs of 'unhappy trees' rescued from the Orangery.

Today the Temperate House is laid out according to Burton's original geographic plan. The south wing and south octagon house African plants; the main, rectangular hall is filled with subtropical trees and palms; and the north wing and north octagon hold temperate plants, such as tree ferns from Australia, New Zealand, Asia and the Pacific. Its sheer size means that it has become the final resting place for many plants that have outgrown their previous locations. Towering above the ferns, citrus trees and date palms in the central section is that king of the jungle, the Chilean wine palm (*Jubaea chilensis*), which stands more than 17 metres (56 feet) high. The species' impressive stature failed to impress Charles Darwin when he saw several growing in the wild in Chile in the

OPPOSITE: Tree ferns frame the spiral staircase in the Temperate House.

1830s. 'These palms are, for their family, very ugly trees,' he wrote in *Voyage of the Beagle*.

The Temperate House contains many plants that have become economically valuable. These include cinchona, from which quinine was extracted to use as a treatment for malaria (today, malaria is mostly treated with a synthetic form of quinine, although in areas where the parasite has developed a resistance to the synthetic drug, quinine is still used); *Camellia sinensis*, or tea; and the coffin tree (*Taiwania cryptomerioides*), an evergreen conifer with a flaking red bark, the resinous wood of which is used by the Taiwanese for making coffins. The glasshouse also contains the rarest plant in the world – *Encephalartos woodii*. Only one plant of this species was ever found growing in the wild. John Medley Wood, who was director of the Natal Government Herbarium, discovered the solitary male plant in Zululand in southern Africa in 1895. He collected three of its four main stems and this became the source of all the plants presently in botanic gardens around the world. Kew received one stem in 1899, which gave rise to the 3-metre (10-foot) trunk crowned by curving stems of stiff, elongated leaves that sits inside the entrance to the south wing today.

Dave Cooke, manager of the Temperate House, takes the job of caring for the world's rarest plant in his stride. 'I'm keen on palms and cycads and I like looking after the old plants collected by long-departed plant hunters, such as George Forrest and Joseph Rock,' he admits. Visitors to Kew often overlook the historic gems tucked away in the Temperate House because the glasshouse is not near a gate. It was built in its current location in anticipation that a new entrance would be built nearby to receive visitors arriving at a planned new railway station. In the end, the station was built further north, at its current site, and the Victoria Gate was opened to serve it. The construction of the new path, the Arc, will make it easier for people to reach the Temperate House. It will lead them directly from the Marianne North Gallery on the eastern side, up through the Temperate and Evolution houses, and onwards across the lake towards the Rhododendron Dell.

Princess of Wales Conservatory

At 4490 square metres (5390 square yards), the Princess of Wales Conservatory (PoWC) is almost the same size as the Temperate House. Built from mild steel during the mid-1980s to replace a series of dilapidated glasshouses and bring the collection

OPPOSITE: Decimus Burton's great Temperate House, as viewed from the newly reopened Pagoda.

of non-woody temperate and tropical plants under one roof, the conservatory is designed to minimize the energy needed to run it. Its sunken triangular shape, with the roof running right down to the ground, helps conserve the sun's energy, while stippled glass deflects glare. 'We have ten zones inside, ranging from dry cacti succulents and some of the island floras through to rainforest and some specialized areas, such as orchids, ferns and carnivorous plants,' explains PoWC manager Mike Marsh. 'The warmer zones are placed in the middle where the heat is contained, the cooler ones towards the outside.'

Enter at the southern end of the glasshouse and you're in the arid zone, where echiums from the Canary Islands stand to attention and spiky silver agaves stretch out tentacle-like leaves. Heading into the warmer, elevated aquaria, you pass by the pond of water lilies and stroll beneath the dangling roots of mangroves. Then a detour to the right brings you to the carnivorous collection. This includes *Sarracenia leucophylla*, which stands in waterlogged peat, waiting to lure insects into its white-topped, red-veined pitcher. The leaves and roots of various species of *Sarracenia* were used by Native Americans to treat diseases introduced by white settlers, including smallpox, whooping cough and liver disease. Now rare in the wild, the plants are under pressure from the destruction of their habitats and collection for use in the cut-flower trade.

On the opposite side of the conservatory are more plants in demand for their flowers: orchids. In recent years this western part of the conservatory has been the focus of Kew's annual February Orchid Festival. Rather than propagate the flowers used in the festival, Kew buys them in from around the world and exhibits the blossoming newcomers alongside its own. 'Within our collection in the conservatory and the nursery we have 1500 species of orchids, but we mainly buy in hybrids for the festival,' says Lara Jewitt, team leader within the PoWC. 'While Kew is concerned with conserving species, the festival's about showing plants that look pretty.' Bringing plants in from far-flung places can be problematic, though. 'Last year we found palm thrip on the orchids that came in from Singapore, so they got incinerated,' continues Lara. 'Then we bought another lot and they didn't even make it to Kew: they got incinerated at Heathrow. Palm thrip's a notifiable pest, so you have to report it. On one level it was really annoying that we had to destroy our flowers, but we certainly wouldn't want to bring such a pest into the glasshouses.'

Aside from the festival, there's plenty of work to be done to keep the PoWC in shape. Mike and Lara use the autumn and winter to resoil and replant the beds, then in spring they clean out the pools. In the summer there's work to be done outside; recent additions are a show of succulent cacti and a Mediterranean garden. Then, as summer gives way to autumn, it's time for pruning. Thus the cycle continues. 'We're about to rip out the top section and change it to a bromeliad walkway,' says Lara, 'because it hasn't been replanted for 20 years. It will look completely different. The bed will be laid out botanically, with each tribe of the family featured separately as you walk along. It's quite shallow because our office is underneath it, but bromeliads are epiphytes, so they don't need a lot of soil. They'll get a lot of sun there, so they should flower quite well.'

Another temporary new feature in the PoWC is a large mural adorning the northern end. Commissioned as part of Kew's 2006 heritage celebrations, the painting shows some of the people who have been most influential in the gardens' development down the centuries. Historical figures such as Sir William Hooker, Sir Joseph Banks and George III are there, alongside contemporary staff, such as Tony Kirkham, who heads up the Arboretum. Most important of all, though, is Princess Augusta, founder of the Royal Botanic Gardens at Kew, after whom the Princess of Wales Conservatory is named.

The Alpine House

The latest addition to Kew's glasshouses, the Davies Alpine House, opened in 2006. The first new glasshouse commissioned for two decades, it was needed to replace the existing alpine house, which had to be demolished to make space for a badly needed extension to the Jodrell Laboratory. The small but elegant arch-shaped replacement now stands at the northern end of the Rock Garden and is stocked with delicate saxifrages, primulas, tulips and other alpines. 'It's great,' enthuses Richard Wilford, manager of the Alpine Collections. 'So far the plants have responded really well to the building. However, the real test will come when we get a very hot summer. The temperature in the old alpine house often exceeded 40°C in the summer, but we're hoping this will peak at no more than 28°C.'

Any plants growing above the altitude at which trees can survive are defined as alpines. At the poles this equates to sea level, but in the Alps it can be higher than 2000 metres (6600 feet). Generally, the plants hug the ground and thrive where it's cool, dry and windy, so these are the conditions that the Davies glasshouse has been designed to imitate. Rather than use energy-guzzling air conditioning and wind pumps to do so, the architects incorporated passive design features to re-create chilly, blustery conditions. 'The main function of an alpine house is to keep plants dry, but as soon as you put a glass roof over anything it starts getting hot,' says Richard. 'As alpines don't like being hot, the design is primarily about keeping them cool, even though they're covered in glass.'

The most obvious thing about the design is the height. Although the glasshouse is less than 16 metres (50 feet) long, its arched roof extends 10 metres (33 feet) above the ground. This is to create a 'stack effect'. With permanent openings at either end, plus vents around the sides and in the roof, the building expels rising warm air and draws in cool air in the way a fireplace does. Cold air is also introduced to the glasshouse via a series of steel pipes. Below the ground a single fan blows air through a concrete labyrinth and into the pipes. On its tortuous journey through the labyrinth, the air temperature drops by two or three degrees. Then the air flows up through the pipes and blows across the plants like a chilly mountain breeze.

The glasshouse is designed to let in as much light as possible, without overheating its inhabitants. The 211 panes of glass have a low iron content that allows 90 per cent of ultraviolet light to pass through. The panes are attached using thin, high-tension cables, so there are no light-blocking glazing bars. On very sunny days, when there's a danger that the inside temperature may become too high, fan-like shades can be drawn across the elongated eastern and western sides. 'The shades will eventually operate automatically once the light level and temperature reach a certain point, but for the moment we're activating them manually to try and work out the best compromise of light and temperature,' says Richard.

The landscaping in the Davies Alpine House complements that of the sunken Rock Garden beyond, where alpines that are more water-tolerant thrive around a pond and among waterfalls. Large boulders of Sussex sandstone form low, rocky shelves and a small cliff, the latter designed to emulate the sunny southern rock faces and shaded northern ones that occur naturally in upland areas. The plants on display come from a wide geographical area. The red-flowered and silvery-leafed *Helichrysum meyeri-johannis*, which grows wild in the mountains of Kenya, Uganda and Tanzania, flourishes beside the delicate British brittle bladder fern (*Cystopteris fragilis*) and tiny-leafed clumps of *Draba rigida* from Turkey. Kew's nursery has some 7000 alpines, but the new glasshouse can display only around 320, so a sand-filled ledge and

OPPOSITE: The small but lofty Davies Alpine House keeps plants cool while letting the sunlight flood in.

Kew has been shaped down the years by many influential people, but in terms of the gardens' architecture William Kent, William Chambers and Decimus Burton deserve particular credit.

William Kent (1684–1748)

Born in Yorkshire, William Kent started out as an architect and artist. In fact, for ten years he studied painting in Rome, where he met his future patron, Lord Burlington. Kent accompanied Burlington back to London and went on to build furniture and temples for him and his friends. From 1729 Kent was engaged by Queen Caroline at Richmond to design garden buildings, such as the Hermitage and Merlin's Cave (see page 178). In 1732 he was also employed by Frederick, Prince of Wales, to renovate the house he had leased at Kew, just to the south of the present Kew Palace. In addition to giving it a new interior and extra wings, Kent gave it a white stucco façade, from which came its name – the White House.

Kent also worked on other houses and gardens, including Holkham Hall in Norfolk, Carlton House in central London and Stowe in Buckinghamshire. He played an important role in introducing Palladian architecture to Britain and developing the natural style of English landscape gardening. He pictured the landscape as a classical painting carefully arranged to maximize the artistic effects of light, shape and colour. 'All gardening is a landscape painting,' he said.

Sir William Chambers (1723–96)

Born in Sweden and educated in England, William Chambers later worked for the Swedish East India Company. During that time he visited many exotic places, and in Canton sketched Chinese buildings. He later studied architecture in Paris and Italy. In 1757 he became architectural tutor to the Prince of Wales (the future George III), and was engaged as architect at Kew by Princess Augusta. Chambers designed more than 25 buildings for Kew, including the Mosque, the Alhambra, a Palladian bridge, the Great Stove and a menagerie, all of which have long since disappeared. Still standing are the Orangery, the Ruined Arch, the Temple of Bellona and the Temple of Aeolus. The most famous of Chambers' buildings at Kew today is the ten-storey Pagoda, which was influenced by his travels in China. He published a book of drawings in 1763 entitled *Plans, elevations, sections and perspective views of the gardens and buildings at Kew in Surrey* (see opposite).

Decimus Burton (1800–81)

The son of a London builder, Decimus Burton trained as an architect and enjoyed early success when designs he submitted for the Colosseum in Regent's Park were accepted when he was only 23. In 1825 he was appointed by the government to carry out improvements in Hyde Park, which included erecting the façade and triumphal arch at Hyde Park Corner. Burton also designed the first zoological gardens in Regent's Park, and Charing Cross Hospital.

His involvement with Kew started in 1840 and lasted 30 years. He initially designed layouts, including paths, a terrace and a mound formed of material from the lake, plus a medieval garden and a rose garden. Burton's most notable feature at Kew is the Palm House, designed and built with Richard Turner between 1844 and 1848. At that time it was the largest glasshouse in the world. Its record-breaking size was later surpassed by Burton's Temperate House, commissioned to house plants from Australia, Central and South America and the Himalayas. It was started in 1862, but was not completed until 1897/8 due to lack of funds, although a section opened to the public in 1863. Other contributions from Burton include the Waterlily House, completed in 1852, and the huge wrought-iron gates that welcome visitors at the Victoria Gate entrance.

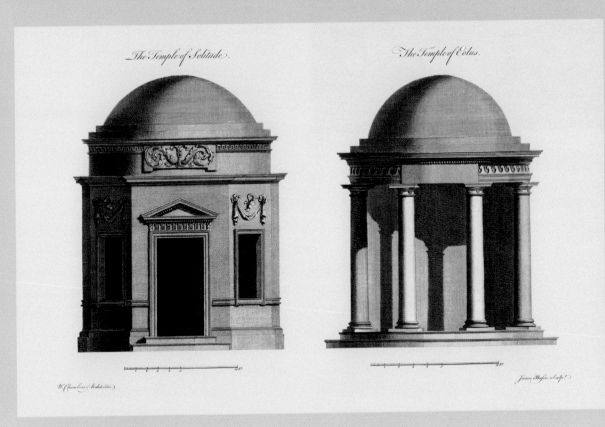

two benches allow Richard and his team to display additional species in pots when they are in bloom.

In the wild most alpines are covered in snow in winter, so they become dormant. The warmer temperatures of west London mean that Kew's alpines continue to grow, and Richard has to battle to keep them healthy and prevent them becoming leggy. 'We have artificial lights we use in winter to boost the daylight and keep the plants as much in character as we can,' he says. 'We have to compensate for the fact that they haven't gone dormant. When it's dull and humid they sit there and try to grow, and get a bit weak and floppy, so we have to give them as much light and ventilation as possible. Then, when March and April come around, they'll just burst into life again.'

ABOVE: Plants such as these *Colchicum kesseiringii* x *luteum* are to be found in the Alpine House.

OPPOSITE: The Pagoda was originally one of a trio of eastern-inspired follies but the flanking Mosque and Alhambra are long gone.

The Pagoda

Rising needle-like at the point where the Cedar and Pagoda vistas meet at the southeast corner of Kew, the Pagoda was designed by Sir William Chambers in 1762 as a surprise for Princess Augusta. It was said at the time to be the most accurate imitation of a Chinese building in Europe. However, genuine Chinese pagodas have an odd number of storeys, while this one has ten. The ground floor is 7.8 metres (26 feet) in diameter and 5.4 metres (18 feet) high; each successive floor diminishes by 30 centimetres (12 inches) in diameter and height. Standing 49 metres (163 feet) tall, the octagonal building was originally decorated with 80 gilded wooden dragons, but these had disappeared by 1813. The Chippendale-like railings around each balcony were initially painted blue and red, with red also applied to the undersides of the roofs. A gilded finial topped the construction.

Unlike many of Chambers' follies, the Pagoda is built from brick. This is fortunate, as the structure's durability has been tested on several occasions. When botanist Daniel Solander saw it during the summer of 1761, he voiced widely held concerns about its stability.

> All thought that a building so much out of proportion should have fallen down before it was finished & no one believed it wd stand the terrible thunderstorms and tempests which we experienced there a month ago, & which were more severe than had ever been remembered. The Pagoda is now considered a masterpiece of art which in fact has stood these shocks so well.

The tower also survived without damage when several German bombs fell near it in 1941. At the time, Allied bomb designers were using the Pagoda to test models of their latest inventions by dropping them from top to bottom through holes cut in the floors, so that they could study their flight.

Although the work of William Chambers' bricklayer Solomon Brown has stood the test of time, other parts have proved less durable. In 1784 a coppersmith and tiler were called in to replace the iron roof tiles with slates, and by 1915 the Pagoda was topped by its seventh finial. Repairs had been needed when William Hooker took over as director of Kew in 1841, so he asked architect Decimus Burton to submit recommendations for the renovations. Burton wanted to replace the slate roofs with copper or cement, and reinstate the dragons. However, his estimate of £3500 was considered too high to warrant the work being carried out. Hooker tried again, unsuccessfully, to institute repairs in 1856. As recently as 1979 the idea of replacing the dragons was again mooted, but as yet the creatures remain elusive.

As part of its 2006 Heritage Year celebrations, Kew redecorated part of the inside of the Pagoda and opened the building to the public for the first time in decades. Each floor has round-headed windows on four of its eight sides, so you are treated to 360-degree views as you wind up the wooden spiral staircase. By the second storey you're on a level with the tops of all but the tallest trees; by the sixth, the Temperate House and Evolution House are laid out in plan before you, and the bubble roof of the great conservatory at Syon Park peeps through the trees in the distance. When you reach the top, which has windows on all sides, you can make out the inverted triangle of the control tower at Heathrow airport to the west, the faint curve of the Chiltern

Hills to the north, the houses of Richmond to the south and that modern-day equivalent of the Pagoda, 1 Canada Square, to the east.

Kew Palace

The former royal residence of Kew Palace is also now open to the public after a decade of renovations. Its history dates back to the early seventeenth century, when Kew became the desirable neighbourhood for an up-and-coming class of wealthy merchants. One such trader, Samuel Fortrey, rented a Tudor lodge at Kew, and later commissioned a palace to be built on the land. With its Flemish bond brickwork and curved gables, the building was dubbed the 'Dutch House' in the nineteenth century, amid rumours that it had been transported from Holland. In fact, the style simply reflects what was fashionable in London at that time.

When George II came to the throne in 1727, he and his wife Caroline were living at Richmond Lodge. Three of their daughters who had previously been living in Germany now came to England to join their parents and three other siblings. With the lodge too small for the whole family, Queen Caroline leased Kew Palace for 99 years to provide a home for the three eldest girls. In preparation for their arrival, the palace interior was updated from its old-fashioned Jacobean style to something more elegant and contemporary. Later the palace was where the young Prince of Wales – the future George III – and his brother Edward were educated.

When George III began suffering from bouts of 'madness' brought about by the condition we now know as porphyria, Kew Palace became a place of refuge for him. His illness, together with the untimely death of his daughter Princess Charlotte in childbirth, prompted concerns about who would provide future heirs. As a result, an unusual double wedding took place at the palace in 1818, when the king's sons, Prince William (the future William IV) and Prince Edward, were married to two young German princesses. The partnership of Edward and his bride produced a daughter, Victoria, who went on to become Britain's longest-reigning queen.

Queen Charlotte's health had deteriorated shortly before the wedding, so she went to Kew 'for a few days'. After witnessing the ceremony, however, her condition worsened and she died at the palace in a chair in her bedchamber. That chair, covered in black fabric and showing the wear and tear of age, is one of the artefacts on display today.

Towards the end of his reign William IV offered the palace to his sister-in-law, the Duchess of Kent. Clearly, she was not impressed, describing it as 'an old house quite unfit for the Princess [Victoria] and me to occupy, being very inadequate in accommodation and also almost destitute of furniture'.

For 15 years the palace stood empty. Although in 1844 Queen Victoria left her children there for a short time to get some country air, it was never again used as a royal residence. In 1898 she gave the palace to Kew for use as a public museum, and it opened the same year. Originally shown almost empty of furnishings, its interior displays were enhanced in the 1950s and 1960s, and a late-seventeenth-century garden was created outside. Structural problems appeared in the 1980s and prompted the palace's closure in 1996 for a decade of renovation and repair.

Modern surveying methods employed during the refurbishment have helped reveal previously unseen features, such as ritual protection marks etched in the roof timbers by superstitious inhabitants to ward off evil spirits. Meanwhile, scientific analysis of

BELOW: The gardens behind Kew Palace are planted in typical seventeenth-century style.

past paint and wallpaper layers enabled the current managers of the palace (Historic Royal Palaces) to create a more authentic decor. Now returned to its original orange and stone exterior hues, the palace is immediately noticeable to visitors strolling in from the main gate. Inside, the carefully researched artefacts, including paintings of Kew dating from 1759, reflect the time when the palace was last in the public eye – throughout the madness of King George.

> The King has so far regained his strength and spirits as to walk about the apartments of the Palace, and to converse with his family. At the latter end of the week it is proposed that the Royal Family should remove to Kew where they will reside in the house formerly allotted to the Prince of Wales, as the Palace at Kew is rebuilding. His Majesty is very anxious to go to the country.

The Times, 9 March 1801

Kew's archives contain many references to and drawings of buildings that no longer exist. Some of these are described here. The visualizations of Kew in 1763 and 1882 show how the different buildings came and went over a century. (The information is based on research conducted by Kew's interpretation officer, Christina Harrison.)

1 Merlin's Cave
Designed by William Kent, 1735
More of a thatched and fanciful cottage than a cave, this was a highlight of the Richmond estate inhabited by George II and Queen Caroline. The building was set back into a mound, and had trees around its entrance and a pond at the front. Inside was a library and a collection of waxwork figures from legend and mythology, including Merlin and Minerva. Merlin's Cave was at one time the home of local poet Stephen Duck and his wife Sarah Bigge. Duck was 'Cave and Library Keeper', while Bigge was hired as the 'Necessary Woman'. The pond became known as Duck's Pond.

2 The Hermitage
Designed by William Kent, 1731
Another folly commissioned by Queen Caroline, the Hermitage was built of rough-hewn stone, set back into a mound and fronted by a circular lawn. It comprised three rooms, which contained busts of English scientists, such as Sir Isaac Newton. The central room had a domed roof with a lantern at its apex, and a small square turret off to one side contained a bell. Sited to the northeast of the present-day Azalea Garden, the Hermitage was retained by Lancelot 'Capability' Brown when he redesigned the gardens for George III in the 1760s. It survived until the early 1800s.

3 House of Confucius
Designed by William Chambers or Joseph Goupy
An octagonal, Chinese-style building with two floors, the House of Confucius originally stood on the island in the 3.5-hectare (9-acre) lake that once occupied a large part of Prince Frederick and Princess Augusta's Kew estate. In 1757 it was moved to the eastern edge of the lake, on the spot where Museum No. 1 stands today. The interior was decorated with scenes from the life of Confucius and furnished with items created by William Kent. Brightly coloured inside and out, its roof was topped with a golden dragon. The house survived until 1844, when it was sold and removed. It may have been re-erected in a meadow near Richmond Bridge.

4 Temple of Pan
Designed by William Chambers, 1758
The Temple of Pan stood on land now occupied by the Princess of Wales Conservatory. Surrounded by wooded walks, it was a place of quiet retreat close to Princess Augusta's physic garden, menagerie and aviary. The Doric temple, believed to be based on the Theatre of Marcellus in Rome, was similar to Chambers' Temple of Aeolus, which still stands today. The Temple of Pan was removed around 1844, along with the House of Confucius.

White
House

5 The Alhambra

Designed by William Chambers, 1758

Inspired by Moorish design, the Alhambra was once situated to one side of the Pagoda. It comprised a single, decorated room fronted by an elaborate covered porch decorated in red, blue and gold. The Mosque stood on the other side of the Pagoda, making up the trio of exotic buildings that became a highlight of the gardens. The Alhambra was demolished around 1820. The site was turned into a sunken garden and planted with heathers in 1958.

6 Theatre of Augusta

Designed by William Chambers, 1760

This semicircular colonnaded structure, Corinthian in style, once hosted open-air plays. It was located where the Temple of Bellona stands today, close to the Victoria Gate. It may have been built of wood and plaster, which would explain why it didn't last very long.

7 Temple of the Sun

Designed by William Chambers, 1761

This classical-styled temple was a central part of Princess Augusta's original physic garden at Kew. Comprising eight fluted Corinthian columns with bas-reliefs of lyres and sprigs of laurel, it stood in an open grove at the centre of a new arboretum planted with exotic trees. The circular ceiling was decorated with a painting of the sun, and surrounded by a frieze depicting signs of the zodiac. It survived until 1916, when a cedar of Lebanon fell in a storm and crushed it.

Garden staff then realized it had been built of laths and plaster, rather than stone. Its site is marked today by an impressive *Ginkgo biloba* that was planted in 1923 by Queen Mary.

8 The Mosque

Designed by William Chambers, 1761

A Turkish-style mosque once stood on a mound where the Japanese Gateway is found today. It was grouped with the Pagoda and Alhambra as a display of exotic architecture. Three arched doors led into a central octagonal room, which was flanked by two smaller rooms with domed roofs. The main room was yellow, with the sky painted on the ceiling. Stucco palm trees stood in each corner of the room, their leaves made from plaits of straw and ribbon. Outside were two slender minaret towers. The Mosque disappeared before 1785, and the mound became known as Mossy Hill.

9 Aviary, Menagerie and Chinese Pavilion

Close to where the Princess of Wales Conservatory stands today were once a large flower garden, aviary, menagerie and Chinese Pavilion. An oval area contained the wooden aviary and the flower garden. A series of parterre beds divided by walkways surrounded a central fish pond. An elaborate gateway designed by Chambers marked the entrance to the garden. From here visitors took a winding path to the menagerie, a circle of pens containing exotic pheasants. The pens surrounded a lake with an island, on which stood the Chinese Pavilion or *T'ing* that Chambers had built in 1760.

7

CHAPTER 8
SUSTAINABLE KEW

PREVIOUS PAGE:
Water use is one of
many operational
aspects used to
measure Kew's
sustainability.

ONE OF THE BIGGEST COMPOST HEAPS in Europe lies in a remote corner of Kew, beyond where all but the most intrepid visitors venture. In a moated compound called the Stable Yard, surplus greenery pruned from Kew's trees and shrubs ends up on one of two huge piles, on top of which cobalt and emerald peacocks serenely sit and survey the world. One mound comprises woody material, such as tree branches and old pallets; the other consists of herbaceous clippings, such as grass cuttings and great clumps of the invasive Mediterranean weed *Smyrnium perfoliatum*. Both waste mounds are duly screened and shredded, then mixed with a generous helping from the 52 tonnes of manure that arrive each day by truck from the Royal Horse Artillery stables in Knightsbridge. With nothing more than a sprinkling of water and the occasional turning action of a JCB, this mountain of organic material naturally heats up to 60°C (140°F), then rapidly rots down. A mere 6–12 weeks after arriving in the yard it is ready to go back to the gardens as a mulch, or to enrich the soil around the very plants it came from. 'We make about 4000 cubic metres of mulch a year,' explains manager of Horticultural Support, Dave Barnes. 'The costs of the machinery and wages of the staff come to about £65,000 a year, but if we had to send all the material to landfill and buy in mulch it would cost us about £230,000 a year. So we probably save about £165,000 annually.'

Formalizing Kew's green credentials

OPPOSITE: The
compost heap
provides a warm
perch and lofty
look-out point for
Kew's resident
peacocks.

Although the cost savings are a bonus, the prime aim of the mulching is to ensure that Kew operates sustainably. In 2005 the gardens became the first World Heritage Site to gain the ISO14001 accreditation for sustainability, after auditors rated Kew's performance in ten fields, including waste management, carbon emissions and water use. The decision to try for accreditation came in 2004. At that time staff were operating piecemeal composting and recycling schemes, but Kew's then director, Sir Peter Crane, felt that, as a conservation organization, Kew should have a unified strategy for limiting its impact on the environment. The challenge this posed was not

an easy one; at both the gardens and Wakehurst Place there are thousands of plants to water, pests to control, visitors to feed and machinery to maintain. Everything, from the stakes used to tie up saplings to the disposable cups used in the restaurants, drains resources when it's manufactured and transported. Meanwhile, the Jodrell Laboratory's scientists need chemicals to carry out their research, and the Millennium Seed Bank relies on room-sized freezers to prevent its valuable collections from deteriorating. There is also the question of how people get to and from the sites. Several thousand visitors arriving by car each year can generate a high volume of the greenhouse gas carbon dioxide. No one really knew if it was possible to marry Kew's message of the need to conserve the world's plant resources with the way that it operated.

Sir Peter asked Tony Kirkham, head of the Arboretum and Horticultural Services, to chair a meeting to discuss how the situation could be improved. After consulting various staff, Tony decided that any action needed to be taken on an institute-wide scale, so he opted to try for accreditation under the ISO14001 scheme. This scheme scrutinizes an organization's current environmental performance in all sectors of its operation, as well as outlining targets for improvements.

BELOW: Peat bogs provide valuable habitats, as well as naturally locking away harmful carbon dioxide.

'The sustainability team represents every department at Kew – from Buildings and Maintenance to Marketing, from the Herbarium to Jodrell Laboratories – so every area is covered,' explains Tony. 'We are a green organization; our main role is conserving plants and educating people about that. In the past, organizations such as Kew have done quite a lot of damage. For example, we've used peat, and we still use chemicals and water, and produce rubbish. I felt it was important that Kew was seen to be a responsible organization. My view was that if we had accreditation of some form, we'd be pretty sound in what we were doing, provided we practised what we preached.'

ABOVE: Rotten coconut husks are beaten into coir fibres, which make a useful substitute for peat.

The use of peat on a large scale by the horticultural industry over the past half-century has been highly damaging to the environment. In Great Britain over 94 per cent of the 69,700 hectares (175,000 acres) of peat bogs we once had have been damaged or destroyed, primarily to meet demand for potting compost. Peat is partially decomposed plant debris containing leaves and twigs from trees, shrubs, herbs, sedges, grasses and mosses. It forms where plant debris collects faster than it is broken down, such as in cool, waterlogged conditions, where the lack of oxygen and low temperatures limit the rate at which micro-organisms degrade organic matter. In untouched bogs the peat can be many metres deep, and the lowest layers may be thousands of years old. The preserved plant fragments can reveal stories of past civilizations, as well as recording changes to the vegetation or climate. For example, at Carn Ingli Common in west Wales, records of pollen taken from peat cores record the rapid decline in forests as Bronze Age settlers cut down swathes of woodland. Peat bogs also help protect the Earth from global warming. Carbon dioxide absorbed as the plants grow is 'locked up' within their structures as the organic material turns to peat. When bogs are drained or disturbed, the peat decomposes and releases the carbon dioxide, a potent greenhouse gas, back into the atmosphere.

Kew now uses peat only to cultivate carnivorous plants, which will not grow in alternative material. For all other plantings it uses peat-free compost, such as coir (pronounced 'koya'), which is derived from the protective fibrous layer surrounding the hard shell of coconuts (*Cocos nucifera*). The fibre is used to make ropes and mats, but as workers strip it from the fruits they also remove the surrounding pulp. In Sri Lanka, western India, the Philippines and other areas with coir-fibre industries this is generally dumped in piles, where it causes disposal problems and occupies valuable land. However, the crumbly, porous residue is effective at retaining moisture, which makes it useful as a bulk ingredient in potting media. Staff at Kew have found it suitable for bedding plants, germinating seeds and propagating cuttings, though in some cases the fertilizer or watering regime has to be modified carefully. 'We use coir throughout the house,' says Mike Marsh, manager of the Princess of Wales Conservatory. 'In the beds it's not a problem, but if we're using the coir in pots we have to be careful because they can dry out quite quickly. We have to rewet them quite often.'

Irrigation at Kew

Watering is another area where Kew has had to make changes. With water restrictions such as hosepipe bans and drought orders now likely occurrences in the Thames area, the gardens must use water responsibly. Kew is in the process of installing a new ring main aimed at reducing leakages, equalizing the water pressure across the gardens and also providing a reservoir tank. The last became necessary after Kew's major financier, the Department for Environment, Food & Rural Affairs (Defra), introduced a law requiring gardens using water from the mains to have a 'break-tank'. As Tony Kirkham explains, 'If you're using chemicals and you're getting water straight from the mains, there's a chance that the chemicals could get siphoned back and contaminate the mains water. So you have to install a break-tank to stop the possibility of that happening. We decided to renew the ring main at the same time as installing the tank because the old system had no pressure and the pipes were leaking. This new irrigation system will help us to be more effective with the water we have, and contribute to our sustainability.'

Although Kew has a dispensation from any hosepipe ban to ensure that its internationally important collections remain alive, it must comply with drought orders to reduce its water use. When water is in short supply, priority is given to valuable

OPPOSITE:
Carnivorous plants, such as *Sarracenia*, are the only species that Kew grows in peat compost.

plants, such as heritage trees, important scientific collections and newly planted saplings. Top of the list are its half dozen or so 'old lions', the gardens' oldest botanical plantings, which date back to 1762. These include the maidenhair tree (*Ginkgo biloba*), the pagoda tree (*Sophora japonica*) and the oriental plane (*Platanus orientalis*) that stand to the west of the Princess of Wales Conservatory. Lawns are left to go brown because they can easily regenerate.

Each of the glasshouses has storage tanks in which rain water is gathered from the roofs. It is better for the health of the plants to use rain water because it is generally slightly more acidic than mains water. Only when the tanks dry up do glasshouse staff revert to using mains water, adding nitric acid to lower the lime content and make it less alkaline. A new addition to the Duke's Garden (named after George III's seventh son, the Duke of Cambridge), at the northern end of Kew, is a water-efficient area that displays drought-resistant plants. Sponsored by the Water Efficiency Team at Thames Water, it aims to educate people to use water wisely. In the UK each person consumes an average of 155 litres (35 gallons) of water a day, while in developing countries the average daily use is 20 litres (4½ gallons).

OPPOSITE: During droughts, historically valuable trees such as Kew's ancient wisteria and *Gingko biloba* are given priority over easily replaceable plants and lawns.

Keeping pests at bay

Making sure water is distributed to those plants that most need it is important because stressed plants can be more susceptible to bugs. Today Kew's ISO14001 remit includes pest control, so it must also consider health and safety issues associated with using toxic chemicals. In the past, little thought was given to the environmental consequences of battling unwelcome creatures, such as thrip, mealy bug and cockroaches, provided it got rid of them. For example, in the 1890s the Palm House was fumigated by burning contraband tobacco confiscated by customs officers. The staff carrying out the procedure would stay inside for two or more hours stoking nicotine pyres. Although an effective way of killing pests, it also nearly finished off some staff. A.R. Gould, who left Kew in 1910, recalled being pulled out of the glasshouse legs first by his mate Jack Watts when fumes overcame him. And Captain Digoy of the 14th Infantry Regiment, who endured mustard gas in World War I, wrote home in 1915: 'We had a very hard summer, with several gas attacks that made me think of fumigating the Kew Palm House.'

Following World War II, most agricultural and horticultural operations turned to pesticides to help keep down unwelcome insects. But although chemical treatments can be effective in the short term, scientists now realize that they often create more problems than they solve in the long term. There are many reasons why Kew now limits its use of pesticides as much as possible. For a start, they tend to wipe out natural predators that would otherwise help keep pest populations under control, and bugs can eventually become resistant to chemicals by evolving methods of detoxifying or avoiding them. In addition, glasshouses have to be closed to the public if chemicals are used, and some pesticides kill fish, so are unsuitable for conservatories with ponds. Finally, chemicals sprayed on to vegetation might not even hit the pests because they live out of reach beneath leaves or in crevices. Instead, Kew has taken a highly scientific approach to battling the bugs, the first step of which is to prevent outbreaks by avoiding the conditions that pests enjoy. For example, spraying water on to leaves reduces two red spider mites and stops them spinning webs.

If a plant does become infected, the next line of attack is to prune away the affected sections, or simply hose off the bugs with water. But if that fails, the glasshouse gardeners turn to biological warfare. This involves introducing the natural predator of a pest into an affected glasshouse and letting nature take its course. So if aphids are the problem, the larvae of the *Chrysoperla* or *Chrysopa* species of lacewing are let loose; if caterpillars are on the rampage, staff release a bacterium called *Bacillus thuringensis* to infect and kill them; and when whiteflies invade, a parasitic wasp (*Encarsia formosa*) is introduced.

Kew also experiments with alternative methods and reports its findings so that others can learn from them. In the non-public research glasshouses it introduced Chinese painted quail (*Coturnix chinensis*) to control grubs. These were found to be more interested in weed seeds, so are now considered a useful biological weed-control agent. In the Princess of Wales Conservatory live several brown lizards, geckos and chameleons donated to Kew by HM Revenue & Customs from seizures of illegally transported animals. Although generally unseen because of their shy nature, they play a helpful role in picking off insects that attack the plants.

The Palm House has a problem with cockroaches, which thrive in the warm, humid conditions. Although they are nocturnal and therefore not often seen by the public, they attack leaf and root tips and can harbour diseases. Over the years, several

Humans have long used plant resources to catch fish. Wooden spears, bows and arrows, traps, poisons to kill or stun, and woven fibre nets have all been fashioned from coastal or riverside vegetation over the centuries. But not many people know that British fishermen traditionally used baskets woven from coppiced willow to catch salmon. 'Putchers' were small and funnel-shaped, designed to catch one fish at a time, while 'putts' were similar in shape, but were sometimes over 4 metres (13 feet) long.

In 1995 Deryck Huby, one of the last salmon fishermen to work the river Severn, gave Kew a willow putcher he had made (see below). Looking a little like a woven trumpet, and still covered in seaweed, it is over 1.5 metres (5 feet) long with an aperture of about 73 centimetres (29 inches). At one

time hundreds of such traps were placed three or four tiers high on stakes across the flow of the river. But by 1999 only seven fishermen were licensed to take fish from the Severn, and a year later the last licence was removed.

Willow weaving is presently undergoing something of a resurgence in the UK, although mainly for making domestic baskets or garden items, such as trellis, while willow for basket-making is grown commercially as a field crop in Britain. The almond-leaved willow (*Salix triandra*) is the main commercial species, grown as short-rotation coppice, and harvested every one or two years to produce tall, slender rods. Osiers (*S. viminalis* and *S. purpurea*) are also good for basket-making. Regular adult education courses in how to make living willow seats are run at Kew's country estate, Wakehurst Place.

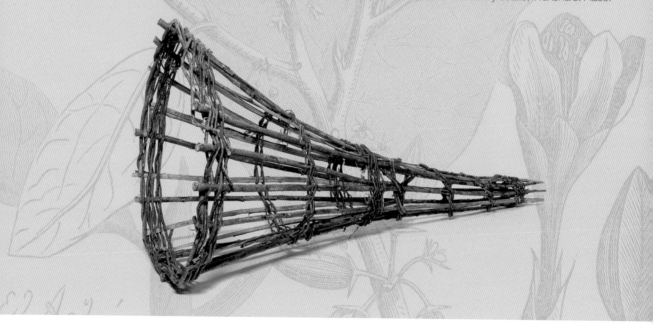

innovations have been made to try to remove the persistent creatures. Researchers at the University of Southampton have created a trap inspired by the carnivorous pitcher plant, which uses a scent to lure cockroaches inside. Once caught, they find themselves walking on a special electrostatically charged powder that gives them nothing to grip on to. The result is that they slide down on to a sticky surface below and remain trapped.

Kew scientists are also researching the life cycles of cockroaches to try to find a way of managing them biologically. For the time being, the synthetic pesticide pyrethroid cypermethrin remains the most effective way of reducing the Palm House population. Treatment with this is carried out twice a year just to keep the numbers from spiralling out of control. 'The Temperate House is often used at night for corporate functions, but our cockroach problem means that we tend not to host events,' says Palm House horticulturalist Wesley Shaw. 'However, we were once approached by the Formula One Jaguar Team, who wanted to "bring their Jaguar into the jungle" and take some photographs of the car. The cameramen were due to be here until 5 a.m., shooting the vehicle against the foliage, but they had all packed up and gone by 11 p.m. I think the cockroaches scared them off.'

Taking nature in hand

Although it has to keep control of some unwanted visitors, part of Kew's remit under the ISO14001 scheme is to encourage biodiversity. In the far southwest corner of the gardens, the 15-hectare (37-acre) grounds of Queen Charlotte's Cottage are now being managed as a conservation area. When Queen Victoria left the cottage and land to Kew in 1898 to commemorate her Diamond Jubilee, she specified that she wanted it left in a wild, natural state. But in the intervening years, the woods and grassy rides had simply scrubbed over into dark, dense woodland that prevented many of the UK's native shrubs and wild flowers from thriving. Three years ago, Kew decided to start actively managing the area to try to encourage indigenous species of plants and animals to take up residence. Simon Cole, manager of the Natural Areas at Kew, took on the challenge of turning the plot into a showcase for native flora and fauna. He is now beginning to get results. Where he has cleared areas of rhododendrons, birch seedlings have taken root, along with foxglove (*Digitalis purpurea*) and campion (*Silene dioica*). Both these native British wild flowers thrive at the edge of wooded areas; in fact, the latter plant's name comes from Silenus, the Greek god of the woodlands.

Like Steve Robinson, warden of the Loder Valley Nature Reserve at Wakehurst Place, Simon undertakes coppicing (see page 130) to provide timber for charcoal, fencing, tool handles, stakes and supports. Some of the trees he cut last winter are already exhibiting healthy red shoots, and the ones razed last year have sprouted thin, leafy vertical branches. Coppicing is a good way to encourage a diverse flora because it lets in light to the ground. The disturbance and increased sunlight encourage wild flower seeds to germinate. When one block gets shadier from the increasing foliage of the sprouting hazel, so another is cut, opening up the woodland nearby. Plants and animals can move easily from one block to another as the conditions change. As well as generating a rich biodiversity, coppicing provides wood that saves money and spares resources.

Keeping up to scratch

Although Kew has now achieved its goal of receiving ISO14001 accreditation, it can't rest on its laurels. The auditors return twice in the first year after certification, then once every subsequent year to check that the gardens are operating as agreed and that Kew is making headway towards achieving goals for greater levels of sustainability. One area that it identified as being ripe for improvement is energy use. It has taken some steps towards lowering its dependence on fossil fuels – for example, new interactive information boards placed around the gardens are operated by solar power, and the new Davies Alpine House has been designed to achieve the lowest possible temperatures and greatest amount of light with the least amount of energy – but much more could be done.

'I think Climbers and Creepers, Kew's interactive learning and play area, could be run entirely on alternative energy,' says Tony Kirkham. 'We could put several wind turbines there, and we could use them as a way to educate children and parents. The problem is, after buying all the kit and doing all the work it might take 20 or 30 years to be cost-effective, but I don't think that should deter us. At the end of the day it's all about giving out the right message.'

MAKE YOUR OWN COMPOST

According to Dave Barnes, manager of Horticultural Support, it's easy to make your own compost. Here's his recipe for success.

- Choose somewhere to make your compost. You can buy a domestic bin, or you can make your own out of a few pallets. If you don't like how it looks, you can always hide it with trellis and grow pretty plants up it.

- Get a half-size dustbin for your kitchen and collect all uncooked vegetable waste. You shouldn't include dairy products or meat, but you can add eggshells and tea bags. When the bin gets full, simply empty it into your compost bin.

- You can put all the plant material from the garden in too, but cut it up first into small bits. You can also mix in lawn mowings, but grass is quite difficult to compost. Alternatively, have a separate box for your grass cuttings.

- If the bin starts to smell it's not getting enough oxygen, so stick a fork in and shake it up.

- You can buy commercial products from DIY shops to speed the rotting process along, or ask a gentleman to wee on it every so often. (Don't use female urine: women have hormones that aren't good for compost.)

- The material will probably take about six months to decompose, but if you cover it to keep the heat in (with a dustbin lid or old carpet, etc.), the process may be quicker. Most of the decomposed material will be at the base so use this when you need some compost.

- When the material has rotted to a fine crumbly texture you can put the mulch you've made back on to your garden. Not only will it save you money, but there's nothing better than seeing what you have made out of what you've thrown away. It's black gold.

CHAPTER 9
FUTURE GARDENERS

PREVIOUS PAGE:
First-year students
taking the Kew
Diploma are graded
on the standard
of their individual
vegetable plots.

EVERY YEAR 86,000 CHILDREN FILE THROUGH the wrought-iron gates of the main entrance to Kew Gardens on school trips. As they gaze up at 250-year-old trees, peer into the miniature world of leaf-cutter ants and experience the nocturnal life of badgers in a child-sized sett, the hope is that they will start to understand why plants and habitats are important, and carry Kew's message of conservation back to their peers and families. Education at Kew, though, isn't just about the environment. Children learn about history through plants collected by Victorian explorers, hone their artistic skills studying the botanical paintings of Marianne North, and stare the future of science in the face among the Jodrell Laboratory's DNA boffins. They can even gain an insight into how maths underlies natural processes, by examining the shapes and numbers thrown up by plant forms.

'Education is hugely important to Kew,' says Gail Bromley, the gardens' manager of Education Development. 'Two key drivers for botanic gardens nowadays are conservation and education. When schoolchildren come to Kew or Wakehurst Place, it's not just about giving them a quick guided tour. It's about getting them to interact, by setting activities so they can discover things for themselves and pick up concepts more effectively. Botanic gardens can be the perfect forum for doing that.'

Kew has 34 teachers on contract, and an additional 33 volunteers, all of whom work with schoolchildren to ensure they get the most out of their visit. 'The only subject we don't encompass is modern languages, although Latin comes into play quite a lot,' says Gail. If bookings are made in advance, children and teachers enter the gardens for free; a fee is charged only if the school opts to use Kew's teachers. The price depends on how much access to laboratory equipment and materials is required, but generally works out at around £2 per child for a class of 30. Schoolteachers who opt to show their pupils around independently are invited to come in for an advisory session, or to look around and get an idea of potential places of interest. There are also information packs on topics ranging from how to use plants across the curriculum to the role of spices in shaping world history and how the Millennium Seed Bank promotes conservation and biodiversity management. For those who are really keen, further material on wildlife and using plants to develop school grounds is available to download from the web.

OPPOSITE: School-
children inspecting
and collecting the
bugs that live in
leaf litter during an
educational visit to
Wakehurst Place.

Making teaching more effective

Kew aims to extend its array of online resources, so it is piloting a new project with this in mind. Sponsored by the European Union (EU), the programme draws on the experiences of five organizations: the Botanic Gardens of Trento, Italy; Sofia Botanic Garden in Bulgaria; the Botanical Garden of the University of Innsbruck in Austria; the Royal Botanic Gardens at Kew; and the Institute of Education in London. Over the next two years each garden will develop teaching materials on a set topic chosen from 'food plants', 'ecology', 'plants in our everyday lives' and 'conservation and sustainability'. Kew is concentrating on the use of plants for food. It will be trying out its new education material on four schools over the next two years and evaluating how well this engages the pupils. Ultimately, all the material produced will be translated into the four countries' languages, and information relevant to each country will be included for each topic. For example, Kew will add recipes from Italy, Bulgaria and Austria to the education materials it prepares about food, and will also discuss how the different climate of each country affects its ability to grow certain crops.

'There will be a website up soon, and teachers will be able to go online and trial material for us and come back with their comments,' explains Gail. 'It's an interactive project because the EU's remit is very much about bringing people together. There's already a strong link between the partners because the person in charge of the Trento work and the botanic garden director in Bulgaria were both students I taught on the Botanic Garden Education Course here at Kew.'

Meanwhile, Kew has been experimenting with some long-term collaborations with local schools. Close to the Order Beds, alongside where Kew's Diploma students cultivate vegetable plots as part of their coursework, two local schools have each been allocated a rectangular bed. One is already displaying a profusion of green potato leaves and tall-stemmed sunflowers. Over the course of the next year pupils from two schools in Hounslow will learn about the relationships between ecology and food as they tend their crops and flowers. 'We're teaching them the science behind soil structure and showing them how to plan their plots,' says Gail. 'They hold them for a year and then eat the produce they harvest at a big party with all the parents. We're evaluating whether having contact with us over a long period of time makes a difference to the pupils' learning. We want to know what their depth of learning is and

FUTURE GARDENERS

if their attitude to plants changes over time. If we don't evaluate our work, we'll never know whether what we're doing is effective.'

One successful long-term project Kew worked on involved creating a wildlife garden at Meadlands Primary School in Kew village. The scheme, which began in 1994, was designed to teach the school's 5–11-year-olds the importance of nature. Kew staff, including a former pupil of the school, helped design the garden so that it was suitable for growing threatened British plants. The children, teachers and parents all worked together to furnish it with shrubs and flowers found in hedgerows, meadows, ponds and woodlands. Today the previously bare schoolyard contains trees,

BELOW AND OPPOSITE: Wooden sculptures decorate the pond in the Wildlife Garden.

a pond, outdoor classrooms and secret paths, and staff use it regularly to teach maths, science, art and creative writing. Meadlands has won many awards for the project and continues to develop new conservation schemes.

Meanwhile, Kew engaged more local schoolchildren when it developed its own pond in the southwest corner of the gardens. Simon Cole, manager of the Natural Areas, worked with pupils at Queen's Church of England School and Unicorn School to design the pond and enhance its surroundings to increase the variety of plants and insects. Today, with its giant carvings of the newts, frogs and dragonflies it attracts, the pond has become a popular place for schools to teach pupils about life cycles and ecosystems.

A typical school visit

On a windy summer's day it's the turn of Kew Green Preparatory School to visit the pond and examine the creatures that have already made it their home. The children form a well-ordered crocodile as they march down Holly Walk, pausing to watch gusts of wind blow clouds of fine yellow pollen from the pine trees. At the southwest tip of the gardens they file past a meadow dotted with blue, white and yellow flowers, before reaching a gravel pit. 'The gravel pit was going to be the pond, but when we looked at it we realized that some interesting plants had colonized it and a family of badgers had built a sett there, so we decided not to disturb them,' explains Julia Welchman, one of Kew's teachers. Instead, Simon and his helpers created the pond alongside the gravel pit, close to where a ha-ha (hidden ditch) marks the western boundary of Kew. Beyond here lies the river Thames and Syon House, the grand London home of the Duke of Northumberland.

After giving the children a short talk on safety, Julia hands out long-handled nets, shallow plastic dishes and small plastic pots with magnifying lids. Working in small groups, the pupils gather at the pond's three 'beaches'. Their instructions are first to skim the surface for creatures, then to explore the water itself, and finally to trawl the muddy bottom. 'Remember to do it in that order or you'll stir up the mud and won't see anything,' warns Julia.

The children fill their dishes with pond water and carefully empty the wriggling contents of their nets into their pots. Each group is equipped with a 'Pond Watch Bug Dial', a circle of plastic-covered cardboard with a water-lily pointer that the children use to line up a creature's features and find out its name. They easily identify a long, thin bug with a three-pronged tail as a damselfly nymph on account of its side-to-side swimming movement. But there's uncertainty about another fast-moving creature that scuttles through the water. 'It looks like a greater water-boatman to me,' announces one boy confidently. 'I've done some research and they swim with paddles, just like he's doing. Look, there's another one – he's humungous!'

After half an hour or so, it's time for the groups to share their findings and gently return the creatures to the water. Julia then explains that it is the combined elements of the ecosystem that make the pond a suitable home for such things as whirligig beetles, caddisfly larvae and pond skaters. 'The ecosystem is everything that helps the pond to live and grow,' she says. 'It's the water, sun, rain and air, and the mud on the bottom too. If we take away just one of those parts, will the pond still be able to live?' 'Noooo,' chorus the children in reply.

Students at Kew

Down at the vegetable plots older students enrolled on the Kew Diploma course are learning about how ecosystems operate from another perspective. The 14 trainee horticulturists are each allocated a plot on which they must grow vegetables throughout their first year. Unable to use pesticides and herbicides, one weapon against hungry bugs is to experiment with 'companion planting', the practice of interspersing crops with plants known to attract or deter certain beasties. So among the neat rows of cabbages, courgettes, tomatoes and mangetout are bright yellow French marigolds (*Tagetes patula*). Not only does this plant deter whitefly, but its

BELOW: Kew has been at the forefront of horticultural education for almost 150 years.

roots secrete a substance that has an insecticidal effect on some worms and slugs. The students have also employed traditional methods to deter birds, including an impressive scarecrow with a cane skirt covered in sweet peas.

For many years the student plots were hidden away behind the scenes, but former director Sir Peter Crane thought they would be an added attraction for visitors, so space was found for them beside the Order Beds and fragrant Rose Walkway. Printed posters at the end of each plot tell passers-by who the patch belongs to, what their plans for it are and why they chose to take the Kew Diploma course. Lourens Malan from South Africa has the worthy aim of changing the way people garden in his home country in order to improve the environment. Less conventionally, Thea Pitcher has sown half her plot normally and half in conjunction with lunar cycles to see if this influences germination or yield. Surprisingly, the plants on one side of her patch do seem to be growing better than those on the other.

Kew first began training up young horticulturists in 1859, when Sir Joseph Hooker introduced a course of evening lectures encompassing economics, systematics, structural and geographic botany, physics and chemistry. At the end of the two-year course, successful students were awarded a written testimonial qualifying them for jobs as curators and superintendents of gardens in the UK and throughout the British Empire. In 1871 Hooker founded the Kew Mutual Improvement Society as a lecturing club for the students. This gave them experience in preparing and presenting papers. After a paper had been read, two other students would begin a debate on the topic, which often went on till the early hours. The lectures were held on Monday evenings, a tradition that continues today.

By 1938 the Kew Diploma course had evolved to include arboriculture, landscape design, soils and meteorology. Then, in 1963, Sir George Taylor decided to extend it to three years, turning it into the equivalent of an undergraduate degree. Today students attend three months of lectures a year, as well as undertaking practical work in different parts of the gardens. 'Within the UK, the course is unique,' says Emma Fox, acting principal of the School of Horticulture and a Kew Diploma graduate. 'We have people from all over the world studying here. Currently, there are students from the UK, Spain, Germany, Korea, Japan, Canada, Belgium, Hungary, France and South Africa. When I was a student I really appreciated the international nature of Kew. It made the world seem a lot smaller and more accessible.'

OPPOSITE: Kew student Silvia Villegas helping to plant the olive grove in front of the King William Temple.

In the first year of the course, students study the scientific aspects of horticulture, including the structural anatomy and physiology of plants, plant protection and soil science. The following year they examine systematic botany, ecology, genetics and amenity landscaping. Then, in the final year, they cover horticultural management and conservation studies. Lecturers are drawn from Kew staff, and include people such as Monique Simmonds from the Jodrell Laboratory and Tony Kirkham who heads up the Arboretum. They also have academics from outside institutions, such as Reading and Kingston universities, and professionals working in industry sectors, such as commercial horticulture and landscape design.

Students have to be quick learners when it comes to identifying plants, as they are tested every two weeks on specimens growing in the gardens. An advantage of the course is that its participants get paid for the work they undertake, so no one ends up with a hefty overdraft. The more enterprising ones also make money from the vegetables they grow on their plots to raise funds towards their Spanish field trip in their third year. 'My year made about £260 on vegetable sales,' says 21-year-old Dan Leighton, a second-year student. 'There was a core group of us that went around the gardens and Jodrell Laboratory selling vegetables, and we also had a stall on Kew Green for the annual garden festival. I was always more interested in growing flowers than vegetables, so I sold big bunches of rudbeckias from my plot, which turned out to be very popular.'

Dan's interest in flowers dates back to when he was a toddler and was given part of his mother's garden in which to grow vegetables. 'My dad's a farmer, and he spent one morning showing me how to sow pea seedlings in my plot,' he recalls. 'Then, in the afternoon, I went with my mum to the garden centre. I saw a tray of pansies and really liked them because they looked like they had faces. When we got to the checkout, Mum asked where the pansies had come from and I admitted I'd put them there. She bought them for me and I went back home and planted them in my plot, uprooting all the pea seeds in the process. I think my dad was a bit disappointed when he came home to find that his son had planted pansies everywhere.'

Dan's interest in gardening continued as he got older. By the age of 12 he had taken over a small piece of woodland around a pond on his parents' farm, and by 13 he had installed a potting shed with a deck extending out over the water. After leaving college, he was offered a place at university to study geography, but felt that it wasn't what he really wanted to do. At the last minute he wrote letters to the education departments at Kew and the Royal Horticultural Society's garden at Wisley, not then

IN KEW'S ARCHIVES: **Japanese paper items**

In the vast chilled room that houses Kew's Economic Botany Archive are drawers filled with paper items brought back from Japan by Sir Harry Parkes, a British diplomat in Tokyo during the mid-nineteenth century. In 1869 Prime Minister William Gladstone requested a report on the paper-making industry in Japan, which was in its heyday at that time. Parkes duly sent the report to England, along with over 400 specimens of paper and paper products. This collection was divided between the Victoria & Albert Museum and the Royal Botanic Gardens at Kew.

We tend to think of paper as being used primarily for writing on or for wrapping things up, but in mid-nineteenth-century Japan its uses were far more diverse. A rummage through Kew's collection uncovers waterproof overshoes that look as if they are made of leather, sturdy toy boxes painted with red flowers, intricately woven hair ribbons that feel like silk, hard hats, umbrellas and even a telescope. Most of the items were fashioned from the inner bark of the paper mulberry tree (*Broussonetia papyrifera*).

Until the year 280 the only paper known in Japan was made from silk with a facing of linen. Then a new kind of paper made from the paper mulberry was imported from Korea. Only after 610 did the Japanese learn to make paper themselves when two priests from Korea visited the country and demonstrated their technique to a son of the reigning emperor. On his recommendation, the paper mulberry was planted across the country and the Korean method of making paper soon spread.

In his report to Gladstone, Parkes outlined the process. First the mulberry stalks were boiled and stripped of their skin. Then the skins, 'divided into portions of a thickness that a woman can grasp conveniently in one hand', were hung up to dry. Once dry, the material was tied in bundles, washed, scraped to remove the outer dark skin, washed again, boiled and finally allowed to rot. Only then was it ready to be beaten flat and made into paper. Other processes, such as adding a paste made from fern shoots to glue sections together, made the paper suitable for different purposes.

Treating paper with a paste made from a plant root called *kon-niaku-no-dama* produced a paper cloth called *shifu*. Parkes noted its durability, observing that ' … saucepans thus manufactured sustain no injury over a strong charcoal heat. Bags may be made of it, in which wine may be put, and heated by insertion in boiling water. Paper thus prepared may be used for papering windows; and will withstand the rain without being oiled. Amusing experiments may be made with it.'

ABOVE: During 2005 Chihuly glass sculptures could be seen throughout the gardens.

knowing that the Kew Diploma existed. 'At Chrismas I got a letter back from Kew saying I was a bit young and inexperienced, but that I could apply as a sixth-form applicant. I had to move fast because the deadline was in January, so I sent off my entry form and only found out afterwards what the Kew Diploma actually was.'

Dan is now pleased he opted for a vocational course rather than a degree, although he admits he is expected to work a lot harder than some of his contemporaries at university. Rather than enjoying summer holidays, Kew Diploma students must work for the whole nine months that they are not attending lectures. In doing so, they experience all aspects of working in a botanic garden, from using tweezers to pick weeds out of pots of alpine plants to mowing the grass and pressure-washing the Palm House windows. Dan's practical work has so far involved making and decorating scarecrows for the Autumn Pumpkin Festival, digging trenches in the Arboretum prior to installation of a new water main, helping to coordinate film crews interested in the 2005 Chihuly Glass Sculpture Exhibition, pruning the Rose Garden and decorating a Christmas tree. 'The idea was that we shouldn't spend any money and that the tree had to be completely recyclable so that the whole thing could later be put in the chipper and composted,' says Dan. 'I decorated it using seed pods, pine cones and dried flowers that I collected around the gardens. I also planted my first-ever trees at Kew. They're birches, so they're not all that long lived, but I went back to see them this spring and they've nearly doubled in size.'

Breaking new ground

OPPOSITE: Kew Diploma students work in all parts of the garden, on tasks ranging from keeping lawns trim to planting new beds.

In their second year all students have to undertake a travel scholarship project, for which they must design and raise funds. Dan had previously worked at Ness Botanical Gardens in Liverpool, and encountered some Vietnamese plants that no one knew much about. When he began researching them he realized there was a huge gap in the knowledge of Vietnam's flora. He therefore decided to visit the north of the country to study primulas because he knew there were lots of well-documented species just across the border in China. Vietnam was reputed to have three species of primula growing among its high-altitude bamboo and rhododendron forests, so Dan went in search of them.

'I ended up climbing the highest peak in Indo-China, and, according to the local people, I was the first person from Kew to reach the summit,' he says proudly. 'I found

If you want to deter pests without using chemicals, companion planting (see opposite) is one way of doing so. This involves sowing among your crops particular plants that are known to repel or attract certain creatures. Some suggestions for effective plant combinations are given below.

Asparagus (*Asparagus officinalis*)

Nematode worms often attack tomatoes, but they can be deterred from doing so if you interplant the tomatoes with asparagus. This also has the advantage of giving you two harvestable vegetables at the same time. The roasted seeds of asparagus are an alternative to coffee.

Chervil (*Anthriscus cerefolium*)

Aphids and slugs can be kept at bay by planting chervil. The leaves of this herb can be eaten in salads, or dried and used for flavouring soups and stews. Dried chervil is a popular ingredient in bouquet garni.

Borage (*Borago officinalis*)

Plant borage (see left) near tomatoes and strawberries and it will have the joint effect of deterring tomato worms and attracting bees, which help improve yield through pollination. The leaves of borage taste like salty cucumber; add them whole to flavour drinks, such as Pimm's.

Dill (*Anethum graveolens*)

Hoverflies and predatory wasps are attracted to dill, and will in turn feast on any nearby aphids. Dill is a good companion for corn and cabbages, and the young plant will help deter carrot root fly. However, it reduces a carrot crop if grown to maturity close by.

French marigold (*Tagetes patula*)

Cabbage white butterflies are attracted to their host plant by smell, so plant rows of tagetes to mask the scent and reduce the damage inflicted by cabbage moths. Marigolds will also attract hoverflies, which are voracious eaters of aphids, so plant them near tomatoes and roses. They are also said to kill couch grass.

two of the species, but not the third. However, I found a fourth species that no one knew grew in Vietnam. We don't know what species it is yet, so it could be one that's unknown to the world, or it might be one of the Chinese species. At present, Kew has hardly any information on Vietnamese primulas, but the herbarium I visited is sending across some specimens I collected with a local botanist. And Kew is just starting up a new programme with the Vietnamese authorities to go collecting and conduct more thorough research into the flora.'

Another student, Keiko Uyama, opted to go back to her homeland to study the traditional art of Japanese paper-making for her third-year dissertation. It was only when she began researching the topic that she realized Kew holds an impressive collection of Japanese paper products in its archives, ranging from intricate paper hair ribbons, to waterproof overshoes. The items were collected by Sir Henry Parkes

BELOW: Many students who take the Kew Diploma, go on to leave their mark in the gardens as full-time employees.

in the 1870s, when he travelled to Japan to study its paper-making methods for the British government. Using his report as her guide, Keiko was able to compare and contrast methods used 150 years ago with those employed today.

'I visited some traditional paper-makers, interviewed them about their methods, saw the fields where the *kozo* fibre is harvested from two species of mulberry tree (*Broussonetia kazinoki* and *B. papyrifera*) and even tried making paper myself,' she says. 'I found that the techniques haven't changed that much since the beginning of the last century. However, the traditional paper-making industry is getting smaller because the practice requires so much time and manpower. To produce good-quality paper you need very clean, clear rivers, so it's made in the mountain valleys in winter. The paper we use today is made by crushing the wood into a pulp. You then have to get rid of lignins [complex polymers occurring in plant cell walls making the plant rigid], so modern paper-

makers use chemicals. That means the paper is acidic and over time turns brown; it won't last 100 years. The Japanese paper-makers use only bast fibres from the inner side of the bark. Because they don't use many chemicals, the paper doesn't brown and can last more than 1000 years. Today Japanese paper is still used in interiors, particularly for sliding doors. It's even used to make components in computers and mobile phones.'

When she completes her Kew Diploma next year Keiko hopes to return to Japan to learn more about the Japanese style of gardening, and techniques such as bonsai. 'I like very small, fiddly work,' she says. And Dan is hoping to expand his experience by working in other botanical gardens in the UK or abroad – 'Although if a job came up at Kew, I'd definitely apply,' he admits.

Eminent alumni

While posts are not specifically created in the gardens for Diploma graduates, plenty of past students have gained employment at Kew. A close look at the parade of mugshots in a corridor of the School of Horticulture's building reveals a few of them. A fresh-faced Tony Kirkham is there, as is Jon Lonsdale, head of Public Programmes and Curatorial Support, sporting a Bee Gees-style haircut. And sharp-eyed visitors will recognize the cheeky-looking chap from Course 7 in 1969. Dapper in tweed jacket and tie is the young Alan Titchmarsh, photographed when he was first studying for the Kew Diploma. 'Alan is our most famous graduate,' says Emma Fox. 'Other notable names include landscape and garden designer Dan Pearson, and Anne Swithinbank, the writer and presenter who's also a regular panellist on Radio 4's *Gardeners' Question Time*. A lot of Kew's senior management also passed through the Kew Diploma course. It's one of the top horticultural qualifications you can get.'

Adult education

Kew doesn't confine its educational activities to school pupils and Kew-Diploma students, however. It runs a range of adult education courses in London and at Wakehurst Place, ranging from 'Badger and kingfisher watching' to 'Botanical illustration' and 'Creating seats from living willow plants'. And its small army of volunteers runs regular guided walks for the public on themes such as 'Medicinal plants', 'Plant biodiversity' and 'Tremendous trees'.

The gardens' educational staff are also experimenting with a range of community projects aimed at bringing together under-represented sections of society. Visitors to Kew in 2006 may have noticed a blue and bronze pavilion standing on the lawn, quite close to the main gate. This 'Temple of the Imagination' was inspired by Sir William Chambers' Chinese Pavilion, which once graced the lake beside Princess Augusta's physic garden. 'We had four groups of people who worked with us on it,' explains Gail Bromley. 'There were Asian ladies from embroidery groups around London, special-needs schoolchildren and adults, members of the Disabled Photographers Society, and a number of A-level students who were studying art at a local college.

ABOVE: The Temple of the Imagination was created through Kew's community education scheme, which seeks to engage people from all parts of the local community.

'Kew Palace was just reopening, so this was a joint project with Historic Royal Palaces. Kew was developing its Heritage Festival theme, so we decided to create a temple based on a historic concept but interpreted in a modern way. The special-needs children and adults explored plant forms at Kew and used their ideas to develop tiles around the base of the structure. Then the photographers looked at architecture in the gardens and took pictures of interesting shapes to re-create in the window panels. Finally, the students explored Kew's succulents area and drew imaginary buildings made of cacti. Their ideas were reproduced in fabric by the embroiderers, and hung in the temple. The overall result was fantastic; we'll definitely be developing more community projects in the future.

'We need to offer different methods of teaching because people learn in different ways,' Gail continues. 'They learn through observation, by copying, by making mistakes and rectifying them, through reading, or by taking things apart and putting them back together again. And the only way we will achieve our mission to conserve the world's plants is by engaging as wide a range of people as possible.'

Index

Page numbers in *italics* refer to
    illustrations

Kew Farm 12
Kew Green Preparatory School 206–7
Kew 100 96
Kew Palace *12*, 152, 175–7, *176–7*
Kewties 39, *41*
kingfishers 134–5, *134*
Kirkham, Tony 186–7, 188, 196, 210, 217
Knowlton, Thomas 13

Lagenaria siceraria 120
lavender *44–5*
Leighton, Dan 210, 211, 216
Lilium regale 100
Lim, Dr Sian Tiong 74–5
Lindley, John 27
Linnaeus, Carolus 13
liparia 111
Loder, Gerald 42
Loder Valley Nature Reserve 128–35, *128–9*, 146
loggery 144–5, *144*
logging, illegal 66–7, 75
Lonsdale, Jon 217
Lughadha, Eimear Nic 102

McGough, Noel 74–5, 78
McIvor, William 33
Mammea americana 117
Mann, Gustav 104
March, Thomas 20–1
Markham, Sir Clements 32
Marsh, Mike 166, 188
Masson, Francis 22, 24, 27, 100, 150
Meadlands Primary School, Kew 204–5
medical research 6, 49–59, 62
medicinal plants 44–65
Melville, Dr Ronald 39
Menagerie 181
Merian, Maria Sibylla 147, *147*
Merlin's Cave 179
Metamorphosis Insectorum Surinamensium 147
Micromorphology Laboratory 76
Micropropagation Laboratory 43, 86, 86, 88
Millennium Seed Bank 43, 54, 56–7, 84, 106–11

Minka House 156, 158, *158*
Monardes, Nicholas 49–50
Montserrat, conservation projects *111–12*, 113–18, *116*, 121
Morris, Valentine 25
Morus alba 160
Mosque 181
mountain chicken (frog) 114, *114*
Murraine, Philemon 'Mappie' *116*, 118, 121
Museum of Economic Botany 30, 36
Museum No. 2 *see* Museum of Economic Botany
Museum No. 1 36–7, 36
Museum No. 3 37
Museum No. 4 37
Myrtaceae family 53

Nandina domestica 160
Narcissus 62, 63, 96–7
Nash Conservatory *12*, 28, 29
National Trust 117
Natural Areas 140, *141*, 143–6, 203
Nelson, David 23, 25
Nelsonia 24
Nesfield, William Andrews 28, 150–1
Nosegay Garden 46, *46*, 47

Oncoba mannii 104
Ophrys 88, 89
Orangery 16, *16*, 150
Orchid Festival 166
orchids 86–8, *89*, 166
Orthodontium gracile 92
owls, barn *133*

Pagoda 172–5, *173*
  design 18, *19*, 150
  restoration of 152
Palm House *40*, *148–9*, 150, 152–7
  early history 30, 37, *153*, *157*, 171
  pest control in 191, *192*
  restoration of 40
palms, Talipot 156
papermaking, Japanese 211, *211*, 216–17
Paphiopedilum gigantifolium 74
  P. rothschildianum 74

P. sandrianum 74, *74*
Parkes, Sir Harry 211, 216–17
Parkinson, Ian 137
Parkinson, John 46
Parnell, Sir John 16
peacocks *185*
Pearson, Dan 218
peat, use of *186*, 187–8
Pericopsis elata 78
pest control 191–2, *192*, *193*, 195
phenology 96, 132
Philodendron giganteum 116
photographic collection 157, *157*
Physostigma venenosum 71
plant trafficking 72, *72–4*
Plants + People exhibition 36
Platanus orientalis 191
Plectanthus 64
Plumeria rubra 118
pondlife 145–6
Prance, Sir Ghillean 43
Prendergast, Grace 86–7, 88
Price, Sir Henry 42
Princess of Wales Conservatory 163, *164–5*, 192
Protea 98–9
  P. cynaroides 111
  P. speciosa 111
Pterocarpus santalinus 72

Quarantine House 40
Queen Charlotte's Cottage 140, *141*, 195
Queen's Church of England School, Kew 145, 205
Queen's Garden 42
Quercus petraea 84
  Q. robur 84

ramin 75, 76
Ramosmania rodriguesii 102
Ravenala madagascariensis 118
remedies, natural 6, 46–8
Remembered Remedies programme 46, *46*
rhododendrons 31, *31*, 42, 143
Richmond estate 12–13, *14–15*, 20, 150
Ridley, Henry W. 34–5

PICTURE CREDITS

BBC Worldwide would like to thank the following for providing photographs and for permission to reproduce copyright material. While every effort has been made to trace and acknowledge copyright holders, we would like to apologize should there be any errors or omissions.

All other photographs by Andrew McRobb
© The Trustees of the Royal Botanic Gardens, Kew.

1 Marianne Majerus; 2 & 8–9 Jeff Eden; 21r and 24 National Maritime Museum; 26 Jeff Eden; 32 The Trustees of the Royal Botanic Gardens, Kew (Plant Cultures); 34 Corbis/Bettmann; 40 Jeff Eden; 41 Keystone Press Agency/Royal Botanic Gardens, Kew; 44–5 & 46 Jeff Eden; 48 Andrea Jones/Garden Exposures; 49 The Trustees of the Royal Botanic Gardens, Kew (Plant Cultures); 50 blickwinkel/Alamy; 59 The Trustees of the Royal Botanic Gardens, Kew (Plant Cultures); 61 Henrietta Vandenberg; 63 Andrea Jones/Garden Exposures; 64 Harpur Garden Library; 70 Corbis/Inge Yspeert; 73 Corbis/Douglas Peebles; 77 all The Trustees of the Royal Botanic Gardens, Kew (Peter Gasson) ; 78b Carolyn Fry; 80 Jeff Eden; 81 Corbis/O Alamany & E Vicens; 85 John Feltwell/Garden Matters; 89 GAP Photos/Dianna Jazwinski; 91 Alamy/Phototake inc; 98–9 FLPA/ Wendy Dennis; 101 Jeff Eden; 103 Alamy/David Young-Wolff; 109 Jeff Eden; 111 Garden World Images/Christopher Fairweather; 115 & 116 Carolyn Fry; 119 Andrea Jones/Garden Exposures; 121 The Trustees of the Royal Botanic Gardens, Kew (Martyn Powell); 122–3 NHPA/Martin Harvey; 128–9, 130, 131 & 132 The Trustees of the Royal Botanic Gardens, Kew (Stephen Robinson); 133 Richard Taylor-Jones; 134 Alamy/ Juniors Bildarchiv; 139, 142 & 144 The Trustees of the Royal Botanic Gardens, Kew (Stephen Robinson); 146 The Trustees of the Royal Botanic Gardens, Kew (Peter Gasson); 148–9 & 151 Jeff Eden; 158 Andrea Jones/Garden Exposures; 161, 164–5 & 169 Jeff Eden; 176–7 Andrea Jones/Garden Exposures; 185 Jeff Eden; 186 Alamy/ Mike Kipling; 187 Corbis/Lindsay Hebberd; 189 Andrea Jones/ Garden Exposures; 203 Jeff Eden; 211 Alamy/Paul Springett; 214 Andrea Jones/Garden Exposures; 219 Jeff Eden.

Page 1: *Dactylorhiza majalis*, a marsh or spotted orchid.
Page 2: Planting beds beside the Palm House.
Page 4: Chihuly glass sculptures in the Princess of Wales Conservatory in 2006.

This book is published to accompany the television series entitled *A New Year at Kew*, first broadcast on BBC2 in 2007
Executive producer: Clare Paterson
Series producer: Deborah Perkin

3 5 7 9 10 8 6 4 2

Published in 2006 by BBC Books, an imprint of Ebury Publishing

Ebury Publishing is a division of the Random House Group

Addresses for companies within the Random House Group can be found at www.randomhouse.co.uk

A CIP catalogue record for this book is available from the British Library

The Random House Group Limited makes every effort to ensure that the papers used in our books are made from trees that have been legally sourced from well-managed and credibly certified forests. Our paper procurement policy can be found at www.randomhouse.co.uk

Colour separations by Dot Gradations Ltd, England
Printed and bound in Italy by L.E.G.O. SPA

ISBN 0 563 49378 X
ISBN (from January 2007) 978 0 563 49378 5

Commissioning Editor: Stuart Cooper
Project Editor: Sarah Reece
Copy Editor: Trish Burgess
Designer: Isobel Gillan
Picture Researcher: Joanne Forrest Smith
Production Controllers: Arlene Alexander and Peter Hunt

BBC Books would like to thank the following Kew staff for their invaluable help: Fiona Bradley, Jeff Eden, Gina Fullerlove, Andrew McRobb, Michelle Payne, Jill Preston, Sue Runyard, Monique Simmonds, Nigel Taylor.